GW00738210

Poetry Ireland Review 73

Eagarthóir / Editor **Michael Smith**

Poetry Ireland Ltd./Éigse Éireann Teo. gratefully acknowledges the assistance of The Arts Council/An Chomhairle Ealaíon, the Arts Council of Northern Ireland, and FÁS.

Patrons of Poetry Ireland/Éigse Éireann

Grogan's Castle Lounge	Desmond Windle
Dr. G. Rosenstock	Joan & Joe McBreen
Eastern Washington University	Dillon Murphy & Co.
Fearon, O'Neill, Rooney	Office Of Public Works
Daig Quinn	Richard Murphy
Twomey Steo Ltd.	Occidental Tourist Ltd.
Kevin Connolly	Winding Stair Bookshop
Neville Keery	Doirín Meagher
The Irish-American Poetry Society	Swan Training Institute

Poetry Ireland invites individuals, cultural groups and commercial organisations to become Patrons. Patrons are entitled to reclaim tax at their highest rate for all donations of between €128.00 and €12,700. For more details please contact the Director, at Bermingham Tower, Dublin Castle, Dublin 2, Ireland or phone 01 6714632 or e-mail: management@poetryireland.ie

Poetry Ireland Review is published quarterly by Poetry Ireland Ltd. The Editor enjoys complete autonomy in the choice of material published. The contents of this publication should not be taken to reflect either the views or the policy of the publishers.

ISSN: 0332-2998
ISBN: 1-902121-11-2

Editorial Assistant/Typesetting: Paul Lenehan
Cover Template: Colm Ó Cannain
Typography: Barry Hannigan
Cover Photo: 'Thoor Ballylee, County Galway', courtesy of John Minihane.

Printed in Ireland by **ColourBooks Ltd.**, Baldoyle Industrial Estate, Dublin13.

Contents   # Poetry Ireland Review 73

Editorial/Eagarfhocal: Poetics and Related Matters

I have given much thought to what I should say in my first Editorial for *Poetry Ireland Review*. Should I express my likes and dislikes, outline an editorial policy that will determine my selection of material for the three issues of the journal under my editorship?

Rather than do any of this, I thought I might write down some of my thoughts about where I think poetry is at now, what its problems are, with itself and with its readers, something that might stimulate productive debate, a debate that could be taken up by others in later issues of the journal.

For it seems to me that poetry as an art is in crisis. Poets, as much as other artists, desire recognition. But on what terms? What do poets think about the meaning of what they are about? Of what value are poetry readings, for example? Has poetry a social function that would justify support from the public purse? Are poets as poets of no more social consequence than members of little specialist cliques, like train-spotters or plane-spotters, often consumed by petty rivalries?

Needless to say, I don't have answers to all of these questions. But such questions seem to me to be well worth asking. They are questions I am constantly asking myself. I feel confident that many, if not all readers of this journal, would like to have such questions at least debated.

* * *

Language must now be seen as a human creation with a most uncertain relationship with a postulated 'reality'. This is the 'disjuncture', referred to by Beckett, between conventional language usage and 'reality'. Even the most precisely 'descriptive' writing – as, for example, in science – is not a window through which we perceive 'reality' and to which it purports to refer.

Substituting 'consciousness ' for 'language', one may ask the question, how can one know what exists beyond language? And yet all languages postulate a 'reality', although the nature of that reality will differ from language to language. There is the 'reality' of Ancient Greek and of Homer, and there is the 'reality' of 19th century Russian as we experience it in the novelists of the period. And so it would go on. For instance, the 'reality' of English of the 18th century with all its 'definiteness' and 'precision', as in Pope or Addison. As we engage with these languages and literatures we are conscious of their social or historical construction. We recognise that their 'realities' or 'worlds' are different from ours and we interpret them into the language of our own postulated 'reality'.

When academics say that language mediates, what exactly is meant by this? How different is this from saying that 'reality' is mediated by consciousness? How closer are we to knowing 'the facts' by postulating rather than asserting the existence of 'reality'? Let me quote the following from Russell's common-sensical *The Problems of Philosophy* (Chapter II, on 'The Existence of Matter'):

… it is not by argument that we originally come by our belief in an independent external world. We find this belief ready in ourselves as soon as we begin to reflect: it is what may be called an *instinctive* belief. We should never have been led to question this belief but for the fact that, at any rate in the case of sight, it seems as if the sense-datum were instinctively believed to be the independent object, whereas argument shows that the object cannot be identical with the sense-datum. This discovery, however – which is not at all paradoxical in the case of taste and smell and sound, and only slightly so in the case of touch – leaves undiminished our instinctive belief that there *are* objects *corresponding* to our sense-data. Since this belief does not lead to any difficulties, but on the contrary tends to simplify and systematise our account of our experiences, there seems no good reason for rejecting it. We may therefore admit – though with a slight doubt derived from dreams – that the external world does really exist, and is not wholly dependent for its existence upon our continuing to perceive it.

In the fifth chapter of his book, Russell takes things a little further, summing up as follows:

We may therefore sum up as follows what has been said concerning acquaintance with things that exist. We have acquaintance in sensation with the data of the outer senses, and in introspection with the data of what may be called the inner sense – thoughts, feelings, desires, etc.; we have acquaintance in memory with things which have been data either of the outer senses or of the inner sense. Further, it is probable, though not certain, that we have acquaintance with Self, as that which is aware of things or has desires towards things.

If we examine Russell's language closely, we can see that for all the philosopher's empiricism, he is prepared to accept the dubiety of a free-standing reality. What it all comes down to for Russell is that the 'reality' postulated by empirical science seems to 'work' and that there is little profit in denying its existence.

What has all this to do with experimentalism in the use of language in poetic discourse? Well it seems to me that some 'experimentalists', and not just those of recent times, but also the Surrealists and Dadaists, reject 'external reality' as postulated in their time, and the language 'corresponding' to that reality, and they opt instead for a private world and a language descriptive or expressive of that world.

However that may be, for many people the result of this seems to amount to little, and they may fairly ask if there is another more worthwhile kind of experimentalism, such as that of Beckett, which is concerned with tackling a perceived discrepancy between language usage and the reality to which it purports to refer. Such experimentation attempts to liberate consciousness from the straitjacket of the paradigmatic thinking and feeling which others have come to accept as the only kind of thinking and feeling that has any validity. This kind of experimentation could be accepted as genuinely exploratory and constructive in its drive, and be perceived as pushing towards an enhancement of consciousness and a profounder and 'truer' understanding of the 'world', and is a corrective to the limiting world of, say, logical positivism; it could also be viewed as a valuable exercise in subverting the corrupt language of politics and business.

* * *

How does one go about explaining the difficulty or obscurity or inaccessibility of, say, Mallarmé's poetry, or that of Brian Coffey, to take a poet closer to home? Isn't it the case that they use language in a way to which we are unaccustomed? But in what way? Surely it is not a simple matter of mere allusions? If that were so, the problem would have been resolved long ago. The Chilean poet Vicente Huidobro clearly spelled out his own position: language is not merely referential but also creative; language can create 'entities' – we would probably describe them as aesthetic – which have an existence independent of the external world, and which are nonetheless real on that account. The 'reality status' of such entities, of course, is still a matter of dispute, despite Huidobro's argument. Figments of the imagination? Illusions? Fancies? And how is one supposed to make sense of such entities?

Let me take a poem by Mallarmé to focus the problem. I have chosen it because it has been translated by Brian Coffey and we can look at that translation to see what Brian Coffey made of it. Here is the French first.

Petit Air

Quelconque une solitude
Sans le cygne ni le quai
Mire sa désuétude
Au regard que j'abdiquai

Ici de la gloriole
Haute à ne la pas toucher
Dont maint ciel se bariole
Avec les ors de coucher

Mais langoureusement longe
Comme de blanc linge ôté
Tel fugace oiseau si plonge
Exultatrice à côté

Dans l'onde toi devenue
Ta jubilation nue.

Here's the literal (from the Penguin selection of Anthony Hartley):

Some solitude or other without swan or bank mirrors its disuse in the glance I renounced
   here of the vainglory, so high as not to be touched, with which man a sky bedecks itself in sunset's gold,
   but some fleeting bird coasts languorously like white linen taken off if there plunge exultantly beside it
   in the wave yourself become your naked rejoicing.

Now here's Brian Coffey's version:

Slight Song

What you will a wild
without swan and nor quay
trains its disuse
at gazing I foreswore

Here from the vaingold
high beyond touching
in which man a sky dolls up
with sun-down golds

but languorously coasts
like white linen cast off
some fleeting bird if dives
exultant sideling

into water you become
your jubilance nude

Now here's a combination of both versions which I made to see if I could find out what Brian Coffey was doing:

> Whatever you may wish to call it, for example, a wild (or wilderness) without a swan, or a quay (bank), it mirrors (trains) its disuse in the gazing which I foreswore (renounced) from the vaingold (vainglory) that is high beyond touching, in which many a sky dolls itself up (bedecks itself) with sundown golds, but languorously there coasts, like white linen cast off, some fleeting bird if you, become your nude jubilance (your naked rejoicing), dive exultantly beside it (sideling) into water (in the wave).

What are we to 'make' of this? A colourful sky reflected on the surface of a stretch of still water which is without the romantic presence of the swan until the naked person to whom the poem refers dives into the water. A poem in praise of human beauty, the human nude replacing the conventional swan? If not this, then what? If we say that the text exists as a thing in its own right, that is to say without referential meaning, what kind of thing is it? What 'sense' are we to make of it, albeit in the way we might make sense of an abstract painting? Can a text induce a response that stays exclusively within language? Imagine whiteness without imagining anything white. Does that make sense? It could be suggested, of course, that one of the things Brian Coffey is attempting to do is make the syntax of his English mirror that of Mallarmé's French with an exactitude that is barbaric, foreign to idiomatic English. If this is right, then the hybrid version I have produced completely loses this by looking in the wrong way for what Coffey was doing. Another question.

* * *

For whom does one write poetry now? The popularity of many poets appears to many a matter of promotional activity and sentimentality. The poetry produces a 'good feeling', makes the reader feel, however delusionary, less isolated. Someone else, like us, has felt the loss of a younger sibling. Or the loss of a parent. It is a poetry of accommodation and consolation. And for many readers this seems to be enough. But is it enough? Is poetry, like human life itself, fundamentally trapped in endless repetition of experience, with change occurring only in circumstantial or contingent detail?

* * *

The foregoing is mainly concerned with asking a few, not by any means novel questions. But it seems to me that too few Irish poets have asked themselves these questions, let alone attempted to answer them. The result of this has been, in my judgement, that the bulk of mainstream Irish poetry would appear to have accepted complacently poetic post-modernism without having passed through modernism. Of course I am not suggesting that Irish poets should now be attempting to repeat what has occurred elsewhere. But I think they need at least to be aware of it. Such an awareness, if nothing else, would generate excitement, a quality which contemporary Irish poetry in general seems to me to be badly in need of.

More Immediately
The Argentine Anthology is the centrepiece of this issue. I was fortunate to have Liliana Heer and Ana Arzoumanian as my editors, as well as my friends, in Buenos Aires. Both of them know very well what is happening in Argentine poetry just now. The Anthology they have so expertly put together is a real 'first' for Ireland. Their willingness to compile this Anthology, without payment and under great pressure of time, is a reminder that on the global literary map Ireland does count for something. Both Liliana, Ana and I wish to express our sincere thanks to Ema Coll, Macarena Gagliardi and María Cordiviola, to Fredy Heer for supplying most of the photographs of the contributors, to all the living poets and the estates of those deceased, and to all the translators for their generous contributions.

Note: There are thirty poets included in the Anthology, and that number is intended to recall the thirty thousand people who were murdered during the military dictatorship than began on March 24, 1976: one poet for every thousand peopled murdered.

Michael Smith, Editor

Argentinian poetry: the written word re-cited
–Liliana Heer and Ana Arzoumanian

Liliana Heer was born in Esperanza, Santa Fe, Argentina, in 1941. Since 1980 she has published *Dejarse llevar* (short stories), and the following novels: *Bloyd* (which won the Boris Vian Prize; since then she has become a member of the jury); *La tercera mitad*; *Frescos de amor; Verano Rojo; Ángeles de vidrio;* and *Giacomo–El texto secreto de Joyce* with J.C. Martini Real. She has participated in several international and national universities' and writers' meetings (Ecuador, Puerto Rico, U.S.A., Germany, France, Switzerland, Ireland, Italy, Holland, Serbia y Montenegro). Liliana Heer is the General Secretary of Sociedad de Escritoras y Escritores de la Argentina since 2001. She also coordinates the International Relations Commission and the Commission for the Disappeared Writers Anthology. She is a psychoanalyst member of EOL (Escuela de Orientación Lacaniana), and is also a member of AMP (Asociación Mundial de Psicoanálisis).

Ana Arzoumanian was born in Buenos Aires in 1962. As a lawyer she has worked on Holocaust and Genocide research in the juridical and philosophical fields. She is professor of Philosophy of Law in del Salvador University. Among her works on law, she has published an essay 'La universidad posmoderna', an article on 'Nelly Sachs and poetry in times of the Holocaust', studies in human rights 'Los derechos humanos y la vida histórica', and a study on Genocide-Buenos Aires called 'Más acá de los derechos humanos'. She is a founder member of the Arminian Union of Writers in Argentina. She worked on the problem of the diaspora and the disappearance of a culture, writing an essay on Antigone as a model of resistance, 'La ley que somete a la heroína, o la resitencia de Antígona'. She has published *Labios* (1993), *Debajo de la piedra* (1998), *La mujer de ellos* (2001) and *El ahogadero* (2002). She writes literary criticism for *Hablar de poesía*, a magazine of poetry.

To outline a map of Argentinian poetry we must cast a sharp glance at the meanings underlying syntax. We are invited to explore the origin of myths, and witness them dispelled. We are urged to identify those Argentinian poets who are truly shaped by their own voices, who are guests of poetry.

The poetic voice, with its ability to evoke many tones, is defined according to its different registers: traditional, avant-garde and 'negative theology' (as styled by some critics). This division produces effects of a political nature, as the poetic voice is always rooted in a historical context. There is a constant transference between society and poetry. At the same time, there is a reservoir of words that rejects change, that does not negotiate meaning: that *plagiarizes*, enriches, repeats, distorts, like the morning remnant of a nightmare...

'My Lord/ The cage has turned into a bird/ and it has flown/ and my heart is insane/ as it howls at death/ and smiles behind the wind/ at my delusions// What shall I do with fear/ what shall I do with fear...' **– Alejandra Pizarnik**.

...a way of expressing that silent words sing, beg, confess:

'My Lord/ I am twenty / My eyes are also twenty/ nevertheless they say nothing.' – **Alejandra Pizarnik**.

Argentinian flesh[1]

Cattle-raising country; a whole cow and more *per capita*. A feast of entrails (to Joyce's taste) where 'red meat' is the main metaphor. From meat to the bloodshed of the *pampas*, literature entrails the unsteadiness of urban life facing borders of troopers, of milkmen.

A powerful voice describes an awkward, violent suburb of Buenos Aires; everyday death represents Borges' ideal of courage. He chooses the witness of a sharp weapon for his Juan Dahlmann. To such an extent that 'meat/flesh' is depicted as the desire resulting from a poor diet, or as the outburst of writing, as that passion that tears itself to pieces with rage.

The myth of meat is always present in oral and written language; it describes the deconstruction of a nation which daily wakes up to be slaughtered.

The historico-political making of a cattle-raising country uncovers the other remarkable myth: the barn – that gets grain and gives bread. A country that shelters immigrants and looks after them.

The silo; an underground place to store grain, forage...men. Into such a construction built to store grain, a nameless world is packed. In this emptiness – of names – poetry becomes the powerful voice that gives itself a name.

'Each death is caused by crime,/ here, now,/ it is known,/ you die because they kill you,/ like when bending down, tipping, / you do know what you are doing,/ coming and going,/ and you know it...'
–**Alberto Girri**

An unfaithful grammar draws up its eyelids and shows itself faithless. When the pulpy tongue[2] of the poet escapes from its sheath and brandishes its blade, writing poetry is a great treachery.

Consonance

The verse or 'poetic prose' is written by means of the – poet's whole – body. The crashing hand attacks and turns into a fist. A conflicting force is always a form of confronting the dominant speech of the day. Poetry claims that it is the place of the political *agere*, where its ethics reveal the living essence of desire. The poet knows that an outcast desire with no historical background is self-consuming.

This arbitrary language, not ideal, language of the shapeless shape, of vivid clear graphs, is beyond epics. And even when this

---

[1] In Spanish, this is 'carne argentina'. Carne has two meanings: 'flesh' and 'meat'.
[2] The Spanish original has 'lengua' which means both 'tongue' and 'language'

contrasting language is constantly describing polarities ('up', 'down', 'support', 'opposition'), there is still an unborn, not yet conceived child, without which it would be impossible to imagine our own world, to dream our own writing, the words a poet gives birth to each time he writes.

'To see, not being, happens to be the stanza function. / The stanza: something too far away. / And if there is a potato in the heart of the skull / it can be (well drilled)/ with a stick: without a chance,/ not ever being there/ not ever saying it...' – **Osvaldo Lamborghini**.

The patience of faith
Self-absorption, self-suffering, joyful trustfulness nest in the heart of the classic poet. In this inner struggle, the writer keeps loyal to what he receives as a gift, to what words expand.

'....Someone must go under the stone wheel, like a wheat grain, / enlightened by the moon of wolves, / searching for the sacred ritual of the four elements/ to proclaim his worship for the soil...' – **Enrique Molina**[3]

In classicism, the 'prayer' – unyielding tie with faith – places itself where language expresses tenderness. The pecularity is the verb which 'embodies' itself in a self-conscious subject closely related to nature and language.

'Her firm absence is the best wealth. / I scent myself with her fled flesh/ If I take my wandering closer to her lips/ my heart enlarges like the day' – **Carlos Mastronardi**[4]

While the traditional poets understand the fertile area of language as the in-uterus meeting of affection, its conception and pregnancy, the new trends see in language the 'machine' that ungrains, bones and multiplies; what evolves, turns up or, in the end, disgusts.

---

[3]Enrique Molina was born in Argentina in 1910. He travelled a good deal abroad and lived in several South American countries. With another great Agrentine poet, Aldo Pellegrini, he founded the magazine *A partir de cero*. In 1975 he won first prize in the Buenos Aries Municipal Awards for his novel *Una sombra donde sueña Camila O'Gorman*. Besides being a writer, Mokina was also a distinguished painter. Among his works are the following: *Las cosas y el delirio* (1941); *Pasiones terrestres* (1946); *Costumbres errantes o la redondez de la tierra* (1951); *Amantes antípodas* (1961); *Fuego libre* (1962); *Las bellas furias* (1966); *Hotel pájaro* (1967); *Monzón Napalm* (1968), about the war in Vietnam; *Los últimos soles* (1980); *Ela ala de la gaviota* (1989); *Hacia una isla incierta* (1992). He died in 1996.

[4] Carlos Mastronardi was born in 1900, in Gualequay, Entre Ríos, Argentina. His books are *Tierra amanecida* (1926); *Tratado de la pena* (1939); *Conocimiento de la noche* (1937); *Valéry o la infinitude del método* (1955); *Formas de la realidad nacional*, (1961); *Siete poemas* (1959). He worked as a journalist in *Noticias Gráficas*, and the famous literary magazine of the time, *Sur*. He died in 1963.

'...The smell of vanilla is not there./ Far away is the vanilla smell./ The wee smell of sour vomit over the face of/ plaster and the white heart. It is not there./ Gone is the sour wee smell. It is not there.'
– **Arturo Carrera**

Landscape

A woman, a bird, the street, the river take over the word up to the point of saturation. The brown river, that neck/passage/aisle, doorway of thousands of immigrants to Argentina, pattern of the promise of an unfulfilled return, engraves and aggravates the 'nostalgic' tone of these *pampas*. A river that swallows and is swallowed.

'I went to the river and felt it/ close to me, opposite to me./ The branches had voices/ that could not reach me./ The stream said/ things I could not understand...' – **Juan L. Ortiz**.

At the beginning of the Sixties the poem turns its eyes down and gives privilege to the null degree of indifference: disappointment. Little by little, the geometry of the city becomes invasive. It destroys in frontier areas; in central areas, non-symbolic reality assaults with its dissecting knife. The poet's alert watchfulness is displaced, no longer holding vigil over the landscape that is to die.

'Under the bushes/ in the scrubland/ on the bridges/ in the channels/ there are corpses/ In the threshing of a train that never stops/ in the trail of a ship on wreckage / in a little wave, which vanishes / In wharves halts trampolines seafronts/ There are corpses...' – **Néstor Perlongher**.

Under the stone of the urban design, there are more stones, and under the river, corpses. Corpses later named as 'missing people'. The opening metaphor of a death that returns from water 'processed.'[5] The city dwellers quench their thirst with brown river water.

The subverted subject

Whereas the orphic lyre pacified monsters, oxymoronic lyricism, chiasmus, antilogy, *mot-valise*, and diverse metaphors from the newest trends present the world as a chaos. Once the dichotomy of form-content is overcome, the subject is nested within the space of disorder. The paradigm changes: it resorts to non-sense; where truth was previously claimed, poets try out new shapes, stir up accidents in everyday life.

---

[5] In Spanish, 'process' is a euphemism for the military dictatorship that began on March 24, 1976

'...from nape to waist/ no one knows/ in that shaped nature/ yet; that sweat, indecent prayer/ there is neither rider nor runaway back: nor hundred eagles/ nor perhaps raped vaults nor quick fastening/ neither handfuls of soil in the face'.   **– Laura Klein**

This language subversion causes the fissure between subject and object. What is crystalline becomes opaque, difficult to pronounce, illegible or refractory to the voice.

The poetic game these days is to surpass the challenge by means of meta-images. The new tendency questions punctuation, baroque writing, the use of capital letters, the hiatus that constituted the language of tradition.

Beyond logos

The death of metaphysics empties grammar-relationships; language reveals an absence that strengthens the word as a grave-voice of the thing. The unmodal tone reflects the discontinuity of language, and at the same time generates a terror of emptiness. Mute. Aesthetics of pure pleasure that marks the faith of negativity and its distancing from nihilism.

Negative theology raises the noun as a dissolving limit of the poetic self. That crushing takes poetry out of the book, sending it to voice and body, as public as uterine. The juncture is erected over a sidelong look. The rush to show more and more becomes loss, disrupts sense.

'I have never drunk some chocolate / where to mix salad with so much thankless doing...?/ Where did they go for Don Casimiro's beans?/ Never throw away the travelling pea!' **– Emeterio Cerro**[6]

---

[6]Emeterio Cerro was born in Balcarce, Pcia, Buenos Aires. He created a theatre company called La Barrosa. He published more than twenty books of poetry, including: *La barrosa, El bonchicho, Las Amarantas, El charmelo, Los fifiris, Las mirtilas, Los teros del Danubio, El Bristol, Las carnes, L hambre china* and *La Bulina*. He also published plays and several novels. He died in 1996.

Alberto Girri

Alberto Girri was born in Buenos Aires in 1919 and died there in 1991. He worked on the literary supplements of *La Nación* and *Sur*, and produced more that thirty volumes of poetry and prose. Girri translated many English and North American poets, including T.S. Eliot, Wallace Stevens, William Carlos Williams and Stephen Spender. He is a major figure in contemporary Argentine poetry.

Here and Now, In the Rough Body

I

Every death is by murder,
     here, now,

  it is known,
you die because you are killed,
        as when bending down, leaning,
you know what you are doing,
          come and go,
and you know it,

        you should know it, that murderers
surround you,
       imminent, impending,
in fact, visible, unnoticed,

       and that you are also one,
and it is your turn to wait for them, the face
growing longer with the fear,
your back hunching,
       and the ways
that a body rehearses
to be a victim:
       passion, aversion and confusion,
doubt and dependence,
       and without faith

here where no movements were,
neither to be born, nor grow old,
wither,
        and like a mirage,
a bubble in the flow,
your rough body.

II

Everybody kills everybody,
            who would discourage who?
everybody kills everybody,
        could the stone be persuaded
not to break away from its mountain,
to come crushing down,
                and the tree felled
by the storm, not to fall on us,
        and the worm that is in us
not only to see a meal in decay, entrails?

III

It is known,
as it is not known about murderers
that they ask the one who dies
what was their worth in life.

– Translated by **Ema Coll**

Olga Orozco

Olga Orozco was born in Buenos Aires in 1920. She has published *Desde lejos* (1946); *Las muertes* (1952); *Los juegos peligrosos* (1962); *Museo salvaje* (1964); *La oscuridad es otro sol* (1968); *Cantos a Berenice* (1977); *En el revés del cielo* (1980); *Veintinueve poemas* (1986); *Con esta boca en este mundo* (1994). She won the *Premio Rulfo*, awarded to the most important Latin-American poet in Mexico. She died in 1999.

I, Olga Orozco

from *Engravings Torn From Insomnia: Poems by Olga Orozco*

I, Olga Orozco, tell everyone, from your heart, I'm dying.
I loved solitude, the heroic endurance of faith,
leisure, places where strange animals and fabulous plants grow,
the shadow of a great age that moved between mysteries and
                                        hallucinations,
and also the slight trembling of lamps in the dusk.
My story rests in my hands and in the hands of those who tattoed them.
From my sojourn, magic and rites remain,
a few anniversaries worn by the gust from a cruel love,
distant smoke from the house where we never lived,
and gestures scattered among the gestures of people who never knew me.
All the rest is still unfolding in oblivion,
still carving grief on the face of the woman who sought herself in me,
    as in a mirror of smiling meadows,
the one you'll consider strangely alien:
my ghost, condemned to my form in this world.
She would have liked to regard me with scorn or pride,
at the last instant, like a flash of lightning,
not in the confused tomb where I still raise my hoarse voice, tearful
among the whirlwinds of your heart.
No. This death admits no rest, no grandeur.
I cannot keep looking at it as I have for so long, as if for the first time.
But I must go on dying until your death
because I am your witness before a law deeper and darker than shifting
                                        dreams,
there, where we write the sentence:
'They are already dead.
They were chosen for punishment and pardon, for heaven and hell.
Now they are a damp spot on the walls of their first home.'

–Translated by **Mary Crow**

Joaquín O. Giannuzzi

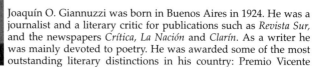

Joaquín O. Giannuzzi was born in Buenos Aires in 1924. He was a journalist and a literary critic for publications such as *Revista Sur,* and the newspapers *Crítica, La Nación* and *Clarín.* As a writer he was mainly devoted to poetry. He was awarded some of the most outstanding literary distinctions in his country: Premio Vicente Barbieri from SADE (1957), Gran Premio de Honor from Fundación Argentina para la Poesía (1979), Primer Premio Municipal de Poesía (1980-1), Primer Premio Nacional de Poesía (1992) and the Esteban Echeverría Prize (1993). He has published the following volumes: *Nuestros días mortales* (1958); *Contemporáneo del Mundo* (1962); *Las condiciones de la época* (1967); *Señales de una causa personal* (1977); *Principios de incertidumbre* (1980); *Violín obligado* (1984); *Cabeza Final* (1991). All of these are included, together with his latest work, *Apuestas en lo Oscuro,* in a single volume, *Obra Poética,* published in 2000.

On the Other Side

Someone has died on the other side of the wall.
At times there comes a voice trapped in a sob.
I'm the nearest neighbour and I feel
A bit responsible: guilt
Will always find a chance.
For the rest of our building
This has gone unnoticed. They speak,
Laugh, turn on televisions, devour
All meat and song at hand. If they knew
What has happened nearby, the thought
Of death wouldn't be enough
To alter the heartbeating of the whole lot.
They would push the dead into the future
And such indifference would be within reason:
After all, no-one dies more than any other.

–Translated by **Jorge Paolantonio**

Joaquín O. Giannuzzi

Final Head

All ideologies thrashed it.
It was humiliated by the world's story
And its country's disgrace, by
Baldness, lost teeth,
Some hollowness dug from under the eyes,
The personal failure of its language.
The workman who had breathed within

– In his greed for oxygen and a steadfast universe –
Let the hammer fall. Reason was
The one that blinded its own windows. But
In Rave found no conclusion either.
Maybe that is why it was not uncivil
In its way of denying the world when taking its leave.
It happened as follows:
Resting on its last pillow,
It turned towards the wall
Those few remains from its face.

–Translated by **Jorge Paolantonio**

Alejandra Pizarnik

Alejandra Pizarnik was born in Buenos Aires in 1936. She began publishing poems when she was twenty. She lived in Paris for several years at the beginning of the Seventies. On her return to Buenos Aires, she devoted herself totally to writing poetry. She published *La Tierra Ajena, Un Signo de Sombra, La ultima inocencia, Las aventuras perdidas, Arbol de Diana, Otros Poemas, Los trabajos y las noches, La piedra de locura, El infierno musical,* among others. She is one of the most admired and respected Argentine poets. Alejandra Pizarnik committed suicide on 25 September, 1972.

Fundamental Stone
from *El infierno musical*

...I wanted my doll fingers to penetrate the keys. I didn't want to pass over the keyboard lightly like a spider. I wanted to sink myself, sick myself, fasten myself, petrify myself. I wanted to enter the keyboard to enter the music in order to have a motherland. But the music moved, it hurried. Only when a refrain returned was my hope encouraged that something like a railway station would be set up; I mean, a safe and steady point of departure; a place from where to depart, from the place, to the place, in union and fusion with the place. But the refrain was too brief, so I couldn't find a station because I only had one train which somehow derailed, contorted and distorted itself. So, I withdrew from the music and its betrayals because the music was higher or lower, but not in the centre, in the place of fusion and encounter. (You that have been my only mother country, where can I look for you? Perhaps in this poem that I am writing).

–Translated by **Macarena Gagliardi**

Time
from *Las aventuras perdidas*

I know nothing from childhood
more than a glistening fear
and a hand that drags me
to my other shore.

My childhood and its scent
a caressed bird.

–Translated by **Ema Coll**

Alejandra Pizarnik

Presence
from *Los tabajos y las noches*

your voice
with my powerlessness to escape the things
I'm watching
they dispossess me
make a ship of me over a river of stones

if it is not your voice
lonely rain in my fevered silence
untie my eyes
and please
talk to me
always

I Talk to You
from the posthumous *Obras Completas*

I am scared to death.
What I feared most overcame me.

I have no difficulty:
I am no longer able to be.

I have not abandoned emptiness and desert.
I live in peril.

Your song does not help me.
Every time more torture
more fears,
more black shadows.

–Translations by **Ema Coll**

Juan L. Ortiz.

Juan L. Ortiz was born on June 11, 1896 in the province of Entre Ríos, Argentina. He wrote only one book, *En el aura del Sauce*, published in 1970 by the Publishing Library Constancio C. Vigil of Rosario City. He died on September 2, 1978.

And it is Pink...
from *La orilla que se abisma*

And it is pink, golden, everything, all the air...
    And the air loses the shore...

A breath, then, from peach trees and from Springs.
    The world?

No more hunger, no more...no more cold, no more for those
                             souls that grovel
    at the doors and in the waste lands?

    No more?
What wet nurse of the islands, celestially, appears
    In the paleness of the river?

Will some children look at her, perhaps, from their hill of ash?
    Will they look at that sweetness that persists
like falling snow there ?

And the little eyes that, for the thorns, scream and scream
                            to the milk,
Will they also look at her?

And of the little spots that are not up, yet,
    to her:
    what?
What, for fear of the blade

or the roads
that close, suddenly, more, inside, the night
below,
what?
What, say, at the moment when everything,
and everybody,
is looking for a way
from the bosom
or for something in the first galaxy, perhaps...
or simply for an echo of that whistle made by some tangled
tendrils of a nightmare
ready to choke?

–Translated by **Ema Coll**

Juan Gelman

Juan Gelman was born in Buenos Aires in 1930. He has published the following: *Violín y otras cuestiones* (1956); *El juego en que andamos* (1959); *Velorio del solo* (1960); *Gotán* (1962); *Cólera buey* (1971); *Hechos y relaciones* (1980); *La junta luz* (1985); *Interrupciones I and II* (1986); *Anunciaciones* (1988); *Carta a mi madre* (1989); *Salarios del impío* (1993); *Dibaxu* (1994); *Incompletamente* (1997). He has worked as a journalist on the newspapers *La opinión* and *Página 12*. He won the Premio Nacional de Poesía in 1997.

from *Bajo la lluvia ajena*

V

of the duties of exile:
do not forget exile/
fight language that fights exile/
do not forget exile/ I mean the land/
I mean the country or sweet milk or swaddling
where we felt/ where were children/
do not forget the reasons of exile/
the military dictatorship/ the mistakes
we made on your account/ against you/
land from where we are and which was
at our feet/ like set dawn/
and you/ little heart that sees
every morning like oblivion/
do not forget to forget the forgetting

–Translated by **Ema Coll**

Juan Gelman

Task

from *Relaciones*

the most difficult task of lovers does not
consist in making love but
in unmaking it to the uncertain
light of early morning or dawn or unready world

do you recognize them when they walk along the street as if
forsaken when they leave
bed and time where they had been together
or like broken torn they go?

you do not recognize them when they walk along the street
as if
forsaken when they leave
bed and time where they had been together
or like broken torn they go

feeling the sudden cold of
so much presence the other and one
only absence and so much
presence the other and only one absence?

so much presence the other and one only
absence and so much
presence the other
and only one absence in
the day of darkness

–Translated by **Ema Coll**

Hugo Gola

Hugo Gola was born in Santa Fe, Argentina in 1927, and has lived in Mexico since 1976. He has published *Jugar con fuego: Poemas 1956-1984, El poeta y su trabajo II, III y IV*, which gathers together some of the most important documents on contemporary poetry. He is the author of *Antología de literatura para jóvenes*, and has translated Pavese, Valéry, Reverdy, Bachelard and Michaux, among others. In 1990 he founded the magazine *Poesía y Poética*.

from *Filtraciones*

3

I HEAR A psalm
an invocation
a prayer
      passionate

I hear the howling of the wind
that struggles
      and passes
I see the sun
sunning
the hand
imprisoned

Everything you touch
moans
and the slow word
says
there is no devotion for anyone

5

YOU DON'T SEEK
the wheel rusted so long
  nor the sign almost lost
  under a sky of rubble
nor do you enlarge
  the orbit
to discover the buried miracle
or to set one's foot better
on the firm shore

you only feel the dream
that comes alone
the exact voice
from one knows not where
the water
the tree
the living stone
that breathes in the middle
of the mud
  of the fallen tools
  that lie in lost orbits
the tiniest animal
the ant
whatever sleeps under the bridges
everything everything that climbs
or awaits
without oblivion

6

THE WINDOW is my eye
more important than the sky
through the window passes
the sky
the colour
the wind
the dense cloud
the strawberry
the dog
the footstep
of the distracted man passes
the plot
of another light comes
the suspicion
the pain
the pavilion of lunatics
that was there
the green gardens
the universe
that wheels and wheels
your eye as well
to see it again
everything

–Translated by **Michael Smith**

Aldo Oliva

Aldo Oliva is a poet, translator and literary critic. He was born in Rosario, Argentina, in 1927. He is the author of *César en Dyrrachium* (1986), and *De fascinatione* (1998).

Requiem

Requiem aeternam dona eis
Domine.
Grant shade
of the living word
to the white hecatomb[1] my gestures wove
about the impenetrable space of the Others.
Grant,

in gentle signs,
real open fires of south sky
to the blindness of my eyes.
Grant, in the fear that fatally corrodes
the passion of the flesh,
the reckless speech of absolute love.
Grant me,
unknown Lord of the Bestiary,
the voice drawn above vertigo,
the flower born of pain,
a splendour in the real.

Ah, long time of silence,
follicles of death unwove
your water under my blood.
Let the hour of the poem surge, then.

–Translated by **Michael Smith**

---

[1]hecatomb: the sacrificial deaths of many people; informally, chaos, confusion

Aldo Oliva

Root

Neither the terebinth of perceptible green,
nor the warm idea of brotherhood,
nor the stars of alcohol
that light up the stars,
nor the luxurious perfume
that worsens the failure
of what toiled in the real,
dreamt, shone, sank,
toiled at the real,
nor the possible number
that strips the world
are YOU, your truth
of the most durable seed that binds
to this gory earth
my hand,
mist, dream,
my hand…
Oh, you, face of dawn,
beyond dawn.

–Translated by **Michael Smith**

Amelia Biagioni

Amelia Biagioni was born in Galvez, Argentina. Her publications include *Las cacerías; Estaciones de Van Gogh;* and *Región de fugas* (1995).

The Panting Unshod
from *Cuerpo en Trance*

she without mouth nor shadow
she in purple green rags
she who lost in the wind her astonishment
she alone on a vertigo footing
by the sharp alien area
she forever fleeing blown up

always hasty twists and
                recovering her bird-amazement
turns over her escape
consuming her in vortex

and on seeing my drawn crowd
she attacks me
unifies me spreads me
hollows me shines me knees me
takes me up
ludic cheerful trilce tragic
forces me to pronounce her
with the breath of her nape

to develop laughing woeful sphinxes
to say her carmine thickness of agonies
to resound her solitudes
     in round orgasm meeting
     in golgotha edge chasm
to sing her wandering dirges
to be intoned remote home
to be exhaled death in Brahms

to whisper her revolutions of Silence
and when sudden
with jump without decline
goes into the enemy zodiac
and another giddy time she flees forever

stays
    half lasting
        reduced
            to crowd in sheet
without me.

–Translated by **Ema Coll**

Hugo Padeletti

Hugo Padeletti was born in Santa Fe, Argentina. His publications include: *Poemas 1960-1980* (1989), for which he received the Premio Boris Vian of that year; *Parlamentos del viento* (1990); *Apuntamientos en el Ashram* (1991); and *La atención–Obra reunida: Poemas plásticos–poemas verbales* (1999).

Eloquence
from *Poemas plásticos–poemas verbales*

Emerson said,
        'I hate
quotes.'
        I don't, we boil
at different degrees.

                There are discourses
on dragons and there are dragons
of hearts.
        What argument
is it worth waiting for?
                (Let's step up on
the trampoline).
        Phrases which support
each other
sleep together; the thing
                – the perfect
eloquence –
is not their prey.
                (Let's jump
off the trampoline).

        The 'wound
of a stain', the 'tridents
of a bird', even 'the cat
which has access to the king'
                are hairs
in the trap.

–Translated by **Laura Wittner**

Diana Bellessi

Diana Bellessi was born in Zavalla in the province of Santa Fe in 1946. He has published the following books: *Destino y propagaciones* (1970); *Crucero ecuatorial* (1980); *Tributo del mudo* (1982); *Contéstame, baila mi danza* (a selection of contemporary North American poets) (1984); *Danzante de doble máscara* (1985); *Eroica* (1988); *Buena travesía, buena ventura pequeña Uli* (1991); *El jardín* (1993); *Colibrí, ¡lanza relámpagos!* (Selected Poems, 1996); *Lo propio y lo ajeno* (a book of meditations, 1996); *Sur* (1998); *Gemelas del sueño* (with Urusla K Le Guin, 1998).

from *Crucero ecuatorial*

VIII

I'll never forget her, Antonia
standing in the middle of the road,
with her black Guajira blanket
her silence and the way
she looked at me.
In the little town of Uribia
I talked to everybody, except her,
the one I wanted most.
Before I went on to Cabo de la Vela
she gave me as a parting gift,
me, the little American drifter,
these words:
        –I don't take off my blanket.
You don't take it off, Antonia,
I told myself, jolting in the truck
with the cans of gasoline, the goats,
you don't take it off,
you don't leave your land, or your people.

IX

When I found myself broke and friendless
wandering around in the city of Lima,
I went to stay at an assignation hotel.
The kind with a grimy façade
and dark little rooms,
that seem to float in fogs
of urine and wind-dragged newspapers.
There were yells sometimes, and panting.
One afternoon I opened the door
on a long, narrow corridor,
and saw hanging on the latch
a stiffened pair of panties
some young prostitute
had left there.
I remember it,
vividly, like a face.

–Translated by **Ursula K. Le Guin**

Leónidas Lamborghini

Leónidas Lamborghini was born in Buenos Aires in 1927. His books are: *El saboteador arrepentido*(1955); *Al público* (1957); *Las patas en las fuentes* (1966); *La canción de Buenos Aires* (1968); *El solicitante descolocado* (1971); *Partitas* (1972); *Circus* (1986); *Verme* (1985); *Odiseo confinado* (1992); *Tragedias y parodias* (1993), *Comedieta* (1995); *Las reescrituras* (1996); *El jardín de los poetas* (2000); *Carroña última forma* (2001); *Un amor como pocos* (1993); and *La experiencia de la vida* (1996).

from *La canción de Buenos Aires* and from *Comedieta*

CITY I

Like the one who
identifies
the city
with his own
tragic fate

crime and madness

Like the one who
has come down
every day
to the city
with his hidden plans

Like the one who
predicts in the city
a tragic plan
hidden
where his fate
is realised

like that one
like that one

crime and madness.

CITY II

Like the one who
has dreamt of taking
the city

and the city was there
and everywhere
and that presence was an
absence

Like the one who
has walked along the streets
of the city
dreaming of
owning her

and the city was there
and everywhere
and that presence was an
absence

Like the one who
has dreamt of owning the city clutching her
in some secret place

like that one
like that one

and the city was there
and everywhere
and that presence was an absence.

CITY III

Like the one who
gasping
in the city
of his desire
went upstairs
and downstairs

until every step
fled under his feet

Like the one who
went up and down
the stairs
of desire
in the city
of his desire,
gasping

until every step
fled under his feet

Like the one who
in the city
of his desire
– gasping –
looked for quenching
the desire that
climbed swiftly
inside him and
went down
inside him
swiftly
and went upstairs and
downstairs

like that one
like that one

until every step
fled under his feet.

CITY IV

Like the one who
feels the city
like a prison
of desire
and searches frantically
freedom
driven

and he was seen frenzied
running along the streets

like the one who
looks for freedom
driven
in his frantic desire
in the city
prison
of desire

and he was seen frenzied
running along the streets

Like the one who
driven
in the city
prison
of his desire
searches frantically
freedom

like that one
like that one

and he was seen frenzied
running along the streets.

–Translated by **Ema Coll**

Rodolfo Godino

Rodolfo Godino was born in San Francisco, Córdoba, Argentina, on March 3, 1936. He has published *El visitante*; *Una posibilidad, un reino*; *La mirada presente*; *Homenajes*; *Gran cerco de sombras*; *Curso*; *A la memoria imparcial*; *Centón*; *Elegías breves*; *Ver a través*. Godino has won numerous awards: Premio Nacional de Poesía (Iniciación, 1960); Premio Fondo Nacional de las Artes (1961 y 1964); Premio Municipal de Poesía (for an unpublished work, 1970); Gran Premio Bienal Internacional de Poesía (1982), shared with Basilio Uribe; Premio de Poesía La Nación (1994); Premio de la Academia Argentina de Letras (2001). His poetry has been translated into English, Greek, Italian and Portuguese.

from *Ver a través*

He Was Split (I)

Woman who is never the same
has turned me into a god again.
It takes place at night, in the pantheon
where dreams lodge,
where the twisted shape is cured.

He Was Split (II)

No-one knows as I do
the partition of the soul.
There is no scandal there.
Only a pause, music
not yet danced to.
It happens a few times, like weeping
or dying.

Echo of the Species

It is not from the body that now flies
washed, made decent, the wounded voice:
in the mind, from the mind
rise the groans
that nobody can fake.

–Translations by **Brian Cole**

Néstor Perlongher

Néstor Perlongher was born in Buenos Aires on Christmas night in 1949. In 1982, having finished obtained his degree of sociology, he moved to San Pablo where he completed his Master's in Social Anthropology at the Campinas University and where he was appointed professor in 1985. His books of poetry are *Austria-Hungría* (1985), *Alambres* (1987, winner of the Premio Boris Vian of Argentine Literature), *Hule* (1989), *Parque Lezama* (1990), *Aguas aéreas* (1990) and *El Chorreo de las iluminaciones* (1992). He contributed regularly to the magazines *El porteño, Alfonsina, Último Reino* and *Diario de Poesía*. He also published numerous books of prose among which are *El fantasma del SIDA* (1988) and *La prostitución masculina* (1993). He died on 26 November, 1992, in San Pablo.

The Corpse

Why didn't I go into the corridor?[1]
What had I to do that night
at 20.25, the time when she went in,
through Casanova
where her rowel rolls?
Why him?
among hovels with glassy eyes,
with thin skin
and those little stains on her face
that appeared when she, eh,
for a pin that her hairdresser left,
started to rot, eh,
for a grip from her hair
in the memory of her people

And if she

started to fade away, let's say
to disintegrate
what shall I say, of the corridor, then?
Why not?
among the fawns with their greasy eyes,
and longing
crouched on the iron roofs, baleful
sweet in their sugary peronism
of that tube?
and what about her gun carriage and two million
people behind

---

[1]The corridor in the Congress building where Eva Perón was laid in state.

at a slow pace
when at 20.25 radios halted
my refusal to come in
along the corridor
reluctant perhaps?
As if dignified?
On his behalf,
due to his agitated gestures
of misery
between his body and the lying body
of Eva, later stolen,
stored in Punta del Este
or in Italy
or in the riverbed
And the story of the twenty five coffins

Come along, do not play with her, with her death
let me in, come on, don't you see she's dead!

And what was there at the end of those corridors
but her scent of decomposed orchids,
of shrouds,
embalmer's scratches on her tissue

And what if we don't take her death seriously, I say?
if we don't laugh among the files
in the corridors and the miles
in the style in which we
did not want to come in
that twenty-hour night
in the immortality
where she entered
along that corridor with the stench of old flowers
and vulgar perfumes
that wanted squalor
we
following her behind the gun carriage?
among the crowd
that emerged from the entrance to the corridors
calling out panic-stricken

And I asked him if that was a demonstration or a funeral
A funeral, he told me
therefore he would go in alone
as I did not want to go into the corridor
to see their feet on the bedside table,
waking up
did I think perhaps of the manicurist
that put on Revlon nail polish?
Or of the gaze of the communist girls,
soaked, yes, and now sick and tired
of losing so much time:
they would have come in along the corridor right away
and wouldn't have lazed around the fringes
fearing the gaze of a blind god
An actress – so they say –
who escaped from Los Toldos with a tango singer
she meets the General in a tremor, and seduces him
she with her ways of an ordinary princess
along a wide corridor
dead now
                    And I
for fear of unimportant
oblivion, of robbery
must I refuse to follow her gun carriage through the parks?
to stuff myself with the transparency of her body?
to go in, shall we go along that corridor where she lies dead
in her coffin?

If he had not told me then that he is alone,
that an older friend irons his shirts
and that he would need, you know, some help
there, in Isidro
where land is cheaper than life

poor plots of land, yes, prone to flooding
near San Vicente (she
couldn't bear the journey to San Vicente
she wanted to escape from the retinue more than once
but 'Pocho' held her back by her arm)

That desire not to die?
does it exist?
instead of staying there
in that corridor with its mouth breathing yellow and stench
yearning to wake up
there, where she rested,
stolen later,
hidden in a large sailor's chest,
where the galleons of Turtle Bay
(sunk)

As if in a game, yet
the thing is I do not want to come into that dark
convalescence, shadowy
– with her burnt ankles
that her sister keeps in a crystal cooking pot –
so as not to lose honour, there
in that corridor
the doubtful goodness
in that funeral

–Translated by **Ema Coll**

Perla Rotzait

Perla Rotzait has published the following books: *Cuando las sombras* (1962); *El temerario* (Faja de Honor de la SADE, 1965); *El otro río; La seducción,* (Premio Municipal del Poesía, 1975); *España en mis colores – Homenaje a Goya,* (Primer Premio en el Certamen de la Oficina Cultural de la Embajada de España, 1978); *Quieras que no* (1978); *Antología Poética* (1988); *Es un largo camino* (1991); *Puertas que se abren* (1996); *Tu cabello de ceniza Sulamita* (1999); *Dos poemas inexorables, largos y con argumento* (2001).

Mutable Poem
from *La postergación*

He had reached the bottom of madness,
that is why he emerged unhurt.
And each day he began the reconquest,
– here is calmness –
and as nothing now could give him pain,
his judgment was clear.
And when he knew that the only
enemy to be feared is hatred,
he stopped hating his enemy.
And his heart also admitted
badness, but never
resentment,
– here is calmness –
and finally chose
duty before pleasure,
for he knew that on the day of judgment
he would have to answer
for that which he did not do,
for not having exercised the notes
given to him,
though he could have done so.

–Translated by **Willian Shand**

Perla Rotzait

The Penalty
from *El temerario*

I have seen you
rise to the wind
and scream.

(Time did not exist
cut into seasons
and that soft murmur
of a thousand ghosts
together
was remorse)

I have seen you.

Among the abrupt shadows
of a song,
in the snow
the ghosts are spying.

I have heard your entreaties
confronting the penalty,
appealing to your judges,
substituting
ghosts for reasons:

To you, remorse.
To you, shadow, dream.
To you, presentiment.
And to you, and to you,
demoniacal horror
of the arbitrary,
of the misunderstanding.

–Translated by **Willian Shand**

Luis O. Tedesco

Luis O. Tedesco was born in Buenos Aires in 1941. He has published the following books of poetry: *Los objetos del miedo* (1970); *Cuerpo* (1975); *Paisajes* (1980); *Reino sentimental* (1985); *Vida privada* (1995); *La dama de mi mente* (1998); *En la maleza* (2000). At present he is Editor of *Grupo Editor Latinoamericano* and of the poetry magazine *Hablar de poesía*.

The Dead Flesh of Language (*In Fine*)
from *En la maleza*

it is your time, they say, never mind
you are dead, or your lover too
her Nobody between enemy legs,

they want your view,
they want you to confess,

they want your contribution, that little out of you
coloured in destiny,

they want your vote, your insignificance,

they want you the way you are,
tame, fornicator, feeble,

someone without imagination,
someone whose time has passed,

someone exactly like you,
identical, particular, unmistakable,
modelled in the manual of leaders,

they want to know you are on the way,
that it is they who are the legendary vessel,

speak, son of a bitch, speak

they want your voice, they want to listen to you,

they want the flesh of language dead.

–Translated by **Ema Coll**

Mirta Rosenberg

Mirta Rosenberg was born in Santa Fe, Argentina, in 1951. She has published four books of poetry: *Pasajes* (1984); *Madam* (1988); *Teoría sentimental* (1994); and *El arte de perder* (1998). She has translated and published works by several Anglophone poets, such as W.H.Auden, Marianne Moore, Derek Walcott, Seamus Heaney and James Laughlin. She participates in the Diario de Poesía Management Committee, and is co-publisher of *Bajo la luna nueva* Editions; she is also a consultant for *Casa de la poesía* for the Buenos Aires City Government.

The Consequence

This is a tree. The root says root,
branch says branch, and on the top
there is the parlour
of a talkative blackbird.

The table where I write
– a spinster's party –
is made of that tree wood
converted by the use and by the time
in the word table.

It is because it blossoms that fruits fall
and for the guild everlasting of its leaves
the tree renews
and the word tree is.

Even though the wood sometimes
hides it to the sight, it contains
the tree in the word tree.

And it is not that this is an abstract poem.
It is because words echo themselves
in sense and meaning: they are unmarried and congenial
and from their roots grows a tree.

–Translated by **Macarena Gagliardi**

Mirta Rosenberg

The Lost Glove is Happy

Run away or stay and love me
when I have finally been lost!

There is no more the discrepancy
of being related to: simply I am,
like the trees
rotten by time
or the old lady that obtains
the bride's bouquet in a wedding.

Lady of Honour, in love you have fulfilled yourself
                                     in time.

Now, I just ask you to share
the useless joy
of being and not being useful.

                    –Translated by **Macarena Gagliardi**

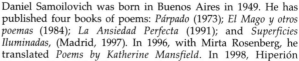

Daniel Samoilovich

Daniel Samoilovich was born in Buenos Aires in 1949. He has published four books of poems: *Párpado* (1973); *El Mago y otros poemas* (1984); *La Ansiedad Perfecta* (1991); and *Superficies Iluminadas*, (Madrid, 1997). In 1996, with Mirta Rosenberg, he translated *Poems by Katherine Mansfield*. In 1998, Hiperión published his *Twenty Odes* from Book III by Horace, translated by Antonio Tursi and the author. His version of Shakespeare's *Henry IV Part I* is also translated, again with Mirta Rosenberg. Since 1986 he has edited the Buenos Aires quarterly magazine *Diario de Poesía*.

In the Enchanted Islands

They mistake us for broom flowers
said the captain; their food.
The land iguanas advanced
dozily toward our yellow boots.
We laughed nervously, false
iguana flowers, the brilliance
of their mistake placing us
in a dubious light.
(To one side, between cracks
in the basalt terrain, you pointed
at grass, three pale threads.
That, you said, was how
life must have emerged, once.
And us the only witnesses.)

–Translated by **Julian Cooper**

Daniel Samoilovich

Porto Dos Ossos

But how can night come if shadows
are unable to cope with the smooth
blue of the bay?
Already boat hulls are black
and the sky is lined with black masts
while water still glistens.
In the bar, silhouettes
the evening cut from silver paper
drink whisky and murmur
in half a dozen languages. And your bottle
becomes like all the other bottles;
their labels unreadable.
But how can night come
if it is trembling
before the blue shield of the bay?
Maybe a swimmer will approach
from the boats, and by the black wake
of his invisible strokes
night will enter the sea. Then, yes,
before the swimmer, night will be here
and the hand with your heart
in its grip will have opened.

–Translated by **Julian Cooper**

Osvaldo Lamborghini

Osvaldo Lamborghini was born in Buenos Aires in 1940. He was a journalist, psychoanalyst and cartoon writer. Founder of the magazine *Literal*, he published *Fiord* (1969); *Sobregondi retrocede* (1973); and *Poemas* (1980). He died in 1985.

from 'Die Verneinung'

...the art of distrusting. It feels good, but still distrusts little.
Copulation with painting is destroyed.
Music, though a beast, has only one back.
Dream is too homogeneous by half.
On the one hand the insistence of the lazybones still lingers,
On the other the stubbornness of the inventors.
Arlt.
A novel of plaster and masturbation.

As every night I went out on my rounds, toilets,
At the cinema there is so little to touch
Like in the homophonic castle of the stark latrines.
Out of reflex: urine
Out of reflex: last
                anointment
Ohm would have reproached fairly
The lack of compact masses in the contemplation
But alive to the slightest chance,
To the slightest sign.

3

'I am your drug dealer'
Mother Hogarth was chained
To a minute crimson stone minute obelisk.
She was placed for abuse.
Any one can inflict a sharp stab wound on her
Or deal her a heavy blow.
Any one can play with her,
She who is bleeding and glowing in splendid contusions.
Semen dribbles down her legs and she has lost an eye,
Consequences of the whip.

All her teeth were also pulled out
To see her ability to suck-cock
Blossom with more aplomb.

But.
'I am your drug dealer'
It is not a consolation, it is a universal prophesy of hope.
And when she sings it softly as a song
Nobody can help but listen.
'I am your drug dealer'

In the district of Once, on my rounds,
I did business with a small cripple and we went together
With caution.
We had to avoid the patrol.

4

The cleaner they seem to you
The waters of the lake
And even when you believe
You are bursting with fulfilment
Still you should remind me
I am your drug dealer

When you contemplate
With upward and pure gaze
At the triumph of cocks
And the defeat of the waves
Still you should remind me
I am your drug dealer

When you go to meet
Your female or male lover
Feeling confident
In the splendour of their pupils
Still you should remind me
I am your drug dealer
And do not walk out on me
Prematurely
Do not behave
Thanklessly
Remind me always
I am your drug dealer

5

To the light of a stolen candelabra
The refined colonel reads in his tent,
His eyes run over the words
Of a French novel.
The confessions are
By a son of the century.

He sneezes, he would rather read on,
But a pang of anguish disturbs him
He knows that if he gives way to sleeping
He will also give way to nightmare

A man will touch his whole body
His hands dressed in rubber gloves

The executions go on, but they are not enough.
The spectacle is not enough.
Even the presence of great masses is not enough
The methodical repetition of death
Does not succeed in showing a watchful aesthetic,
Perpetually insomniac.

And already the icy rubber
Slides over his breasts
And with certainty looks for his penis
And the dumb edges
That protect the anal cavity.

How are bad poems born?
In the dissatisfaction with dullness
When the place of power is stared at
And a blank is seen instead of void
Monosexuality
Rudimentary organs.

The small cripple eats chocolate in a corner of the room.
I call him and kiss him.
His physical sore preserves distance.

–translated by **Ema Coll**

María Negroni

María Negroni was born in Argentina. She is a translator and holds a PhD in Latin American Literature (Columbia University, New York). She has published numerous books of poetry, including: *de tanto desolar* (1985); *per/canta* (1989); *La jaula bajo el trapo* (1991); *Islandia* (1994); *El viaje de la noche* (1994); *Diario Extranjero* (2000); *Camera delle Meraviglie* (2002); and *La ineptitud* (2002). She has also published two books of essays, *Ciudad Gótica* (1994), and *Museo Negro* (1999), as well as a novel, *El sueño de Úrsula* (1998). Many of her books have been translated into English.

The Journey

An image that stems from me, myself, only
immaterial, persuades me and together we leave
the train. We reach the surface, the train under-
ground. Almost at once we learn of the tragedy:
fire destroys a train, thousands die. Someone says:
life's joys are ephemeral. Stunned with terror, I
descend the stairs, return to the platform. In the
red and silent train – now motionless – I search
for the man I love. When I find him, I see his gaze
wandering: there is a dead child in his arms and a
mask. In the smoke, he looks hazy, so beautiful
that I'm about to kiss him. But everything
goes up in flames again and his image becomes
unbearable. His eyes speak another language and
another silence. His eyes, in the shadow of light. I
start to cry. To demand that he recognize me. To
plead with him. The scene convulses with effort,
it could shatter like a glass. I leave. Walk among
burning coals. The beloved, his name
uninhabitable, has lost his mind.

–Translated by **Anne Twitty**

Arturo Carrera

Arturo Carrera was born in Rosario, Argentina in 1956. He teaches literature and coordinates literary workshops. He has published *De cobre y barro* (1981); *Máscaras de familia* (1991); and *Jardines cerrados al público* (1999). Some of his work has been translated into French.

The Family

In the family
picture cut through in
colours

The cut stomach,
the toys.

Why return to unity?

Nature was the imitation of the father,
the limitless gaze of the Mother: and love,
although it was probably not love, claimed
a brief fall over other silent
times.

Claimed the children sinking
in the strenuous foliage,
in the foam of the branches. Claimed everything
that feigned brief lives for itself, and
all the small presence that burned,
all the mysterious nominations, all
the fleeting lies of a few barbed gestures:

the countryside destroyed the pain
which could be perceived as proof of solitude
in the landscape.

Then the stomping,
the massacre of desire: the inability
to reduce to a common maternal denominator
the bad father and the cheating grandfather.

The very sweet look in that night
which would open only for sleep…
which perhaps no longer kept
a rhythm: schizophrenic crickets.

Lovers?

Fascinating body and small domination
The vibration of caresses that still creak
in us like very soft tumblings of light.

Lovers?

And in the happiness of the shouts,
who consented to taking on
a name unique yet complainant?

Who, in life,
in the urticant steam
of an entire secret?

–Translated by **Sergio Waisman**

Susana Romano

Susana Romano was born in Córdoba, Argentina, in 1947. She finished her studies in Modern Literature and Psychology, and then obtained her PhD in Philosophy in Germany. She has published: *Verdades como criptas* (1980, first award of the Luis Tejada competition of Córdoba); *El corazón constante* (1989); *Escriturienta* (1994); *Frida Kahlo y otros poemas* (1997); *Nomenclatura: muros* (1997); *Algesia* (2000). Her published essays include 'La diaspora de la diaspora – Una poética de la traducción Poética' (1995); 'La escritura en la diaspora – Poéticas de Traducción' (1998).

A Question of Degree
from *Escriturienta*

The aspiration retreats and then gives in:
To a standing position the lying down
To a one-eyed the blinded
To a hand the dismembered
To a blow from a stick the mutilated
To a brother the dismothered
To a whisper the tongue cut
To leprosy gangrene
To the ripe rotten
To the human the jailed
To the jailed the disappeared
To a proper name the buried.

–Translated by **Graciela Berti**

Susana Romano

The Lovers
from *Algesia*

II
Pilgrims have no place from where to come.

The pain incubates in the intervals of passion
The afternoon never ceases being afternoon
The trembling does not reach the ground
Between one sentence and another time does not end

Pain breeds
Rough seas of pain
Springs of pain watering and watering the wasteland

The lovers cancel the fear of time
All the watches in the world are set at the same hour
Which is the hour of the wrists of the lovers.

They make the seconds shine and throw golden coins
                                        toward
the universe
and spread the waiting on the limits of the quadrant

The lovers give shelter and care to the mourning
                                        pilgrims
Decorate the beds
And migrate from one mood to another

The steps are felt in the panic
turned against itself as in trimmings of a dream
seen with the images of the day
The rest of familiar things
That return with eyes and bodies unopened

Pilgrims have no place from where to come

–Translated by **Graciela Berti**

Jorge Boccanera

Jorge Boccanera was born in Buenos Aires in 1952. His latest book of poetry is *Bestias en un hotel de paso*. He wrote an essay about Juan Gelman's plays, and another about Luis Cardoza y Aragón. He has published several other books, including *La pasión de los poetas*; *Tierra que anda* and *Redes de la memoria*. He has participated in an Amnesty Meeting against torture which took place in Mexico, in 2000, as well as in a forum against globalisation held in Florence in 2001.

The Rock of the Jail

She turns on the radio hammer and tongs when I try to write,
    when I want to sleep,
    she dances on the upper floor.
She goes downstairs with her heavy tapping,
    her children cry,
    her dogs bark.
The whole blessed day there are people knocking on my door
    and they say as an excuse: I've
mistaken the door.
Now she runs upstairs, slams the door of her room and argues
    at the top of her voice.
    Her children bark,
    her dogs cry.
The neighbourhood with her is much more than a cockfight on
    the roof,
much worse than a blast inside a pillow.
One day I breathed deeply, went upstairs,
A dying man answered me,
I shyly said: I've mistaken the door,
    my children cry,
    my dogs bark.
Her radio is hammer and tongs when I try to write,
    when I want to sleep,
    she dances on the upper floor.
For years my only wish has been to meet her on the stairs
and tell her to her face I'm leaving!
and douse her with petrol,
and put out my cigarette on her red dress.

–Translated by **Ema Coll**

Jorge Boccanera

Adventures

Deaf-mute
we live tied back to back
and someone rips the tent where you are prisoner:
little blue tongue do not cry
outside the horses snort restlessly
and there are several sentries for only one stone.

Oar of my canoe, messenger, your tongue sparkles near the fire
  when we are back to back.
Do not make any noise,
there are shreds of boredom on the bushes,
empty canteens.

Crazy for being gagged, stubborn, captive,
there are rusty nails in your tongue, there are tin soldiers.
I have seen them camping and collecting firewood,
I have seen their shaved heads, their dirty uniforms.

Every night we dream of a glass horse biting the ties,
but it dawns and we keep going back to back.

–Translated by **Ema Coll**

Guillermo Saavedra

Guillermo Saavedra was born in Buenos Aires in 1960. He is a poet, editor, literary critic and cultural journalist. His books of poetry are: *Caracol* (1989); *Tentativas sobre Cage* (1995); and *El velador* (1998). He has also published a children's book, *Pancitas argentinas* (2000); a book of interviews with Argentine fiction writers, *La curiosidad impertinente*; and he has compiled the anthologies, *Cuentos de historia argentina* (1999), *La pena del aire* (a selection of the poems of Ricardo Molinari), *Cuentos escogidos de Andrés Rivera* (2000), *Mi cuento favorito* (2001), *Cuentos de escritoras argentinas* (2001). He received a Guggenheim bursary in 2001. At present he is the Editor of the Sunday magazine issued with *La Nación*.

from *Tentativas sobre Cage*

II

Let it just
go to
its hub:
the end

itself is consumed
in algae;
the deluge
dreams in the desert.

VIII

Buying jasmine
and allowing it to dry,
until the air chokes that proud
whiteness.

Procuring
the aroma: an ancient
plague,
almost legendary.

IX

The job of rising
without moving,
like a horde
in potential

which can never attack
yet all the same
ravages
the enemy.

X

To slice an orange is just like cutting it
all over.
a crime, horrible
and also necessary:

the acid
balance
of segments,
of seeds.

XVI

A project
against oblivion. Not
the humid
disenchantment

of remembrances, but
with the air of
a long, fading
absence.

XVIII

A jotting page:
luminosity drowsing,
a nothing,
and a

grimace,
the tip of a
vague
adherence.

XXIV

A jagged needle
whose
thread
stays in shadow:

stitching that
astutely
engrafts
the invisible.

XXXIV

A long journey
From everything,
thin ice,
unhurried

condensation,
a soul
In its gaseous
intermittence.

XXXV

Jammed
cellophane:
without sparks,
the illusion of fire.

Incandescence?
It's that, on opening, the unwrapping
most aged light
incinerates.

XXXVIII

Jade-green
billows
always hospitable,
do not deny themselves:

the inventor composed, with
aleatoric meditation,
the only avant-garde that's
non-violent.

–Translated by **Julian Cooper**

Note: In the Spanish text there is a play on the name 'John Cage' with a letter in every verse.

Susana Villalba

Susana Villalba has published *Oficiante de Sombras* (1982); *Clínica de muñecas* (1986); *Susy, secretos del corazón* (1989); *Matar un animal* (1995 in Venezuela and 1997 in Argentina); and *Caminatas* (1999). She is director for the last years of the *Casa Nacional de la Poesía* (National House for Poetry) and the *Festival Internacional de Poesía* (International Festival of Poetry).

Unfinished Piece for a Mechanical Piano
from *Plegarias*

So? One should bless in the face of death. Whether white or black. Illusion, object of desire and any symbol that may watch over us, what do questions already put and answered matter, if nothing is known, although one can read, and even when it befalls us once more, bless all that ask themselves again. As though it were genesis, the first man and the first woman parting ways. To bless the naïvety of so many hours, the months spent asking and sitting on ignorance, so. There is a moment when love hits, makes a kill, clears with a faulty godspeed. Then I bless your disgust, your everybody for himself your sacred pot belly and your fear of god. No one attempts a jump he thinks deadly, thank heaven. Which we all know is abstract. Bless then the instinct that pins you to your flat as well as my ignorance of your not knowing what's good for you either. I believe in the father and in the son, in Platonov's wife when she pulls him out of the river as she would a young boy whose shoes are drenched. I believe in the convenience of there having been no flood. I wonder was he aware, what the lover wished, there are things I don't know and never mind how often they were learned and forgotten. Bless oblivion. Bless a love that chases us out of ourselves. Bless the selfishness that divides us in front of the danger of being ourselves another way. And who wanted Eurydice. The poem, the nightingale and not the enamored fellow tinging the rose with his blood. Bless the mud alchemy that sets for a foothold, an idol forgetful of its latent shipwreck. Do not wait on the coast, what the waves wash is always scrap, one just goes back to one's mirage and mine is waiting. No one jumps without asking what lies in wait. Bless the calm, the proffered fruit and a local temperature, the temperance with which one grips the log one has been alotted. Or did one choose?

Ambiguity. Bless confusion, believing one has owned, to believe, to think one cannot own unless one gives. Life as a sea that flows and ebbs, the death of whosoever should slay you. I believe in solitude as one believing in the illusion of a world now lost. So? One must bless as one finds or feels the fitting block in the shelter a child has built. Or not fitting, bless the temptation to upset it all, build something else, ask. Bless the storm that returns nonetheless to the idea of foundering. Its thrust is followed by a sudden bend towards the coast. And who wanted the promised land, a known paradise we'll lose again. It isn't true we knew, it isn't true we caressed the tree, the notion of good and evil wasn't within our reach, bless it. So bless your foolishness and your candour, your arrogance frees you from all charges and bless your ignorance of others. And mine.

–Translated by **Luis Huerga**

Laura Yasan

Laura Yasan was born in Buenos Aires in 1960. She has co-ordinated writing workshops in jails, young people's hostels, retirement homes, unions offices, and libraries. In 1988 she compiled the *III Illustrated Anthology of Young People's Poetry*. Her publications are: *Doble de alma* (1995); *Cambiar las armas* (1997); *Loba negra* (1999); and *Cotillón para desesperados* (2001). *Loba negra* received the Prize of Poetry EDUCA, Costa Rica, 1998, and 3rd Prize from Fondo Nacional de las Artes, Buenos Aires, 1998. Since 2000 she has been a member of the Editorial Board of the literary magazine *Los rollos del mal muerto*, and, since 2001, a member of the Human Rights Commission at the Sociedad de Escritoras y Escritores de la Argentina (SEA).

genealogy

the daughters of the new world
are as white as shopping centre lights
as pale as mcdonald's bread
translucent tears ending best-sellers

the orphan mothers of the daughters of the new world
were seedy hotel dwellers
we viewed the world darkly
we desired life reflecting icons
bergman films

the frigid mothers of the orphan mothers of the daughters of the
                                    new world
wanted to have a story immersed in chanel
marry virginally a replica of cary grant
give birth to blonde dolls with rosy cheeks
who chew gum while reading little women

we, the orphan daughters of the frigid mothers of the new world
wanted the sensual curves of marilyn
and the latin look of one of che's lovers

but they
the grandaughters of decadence
the daughters of the empire of the new world
just want to be
as thin as a stalk
as light as the wings of a butterfly

they long for waking up every day
with their fingers longer and longer
so as to sink them to the bottom of their tonsils
and throw up involuntarily
what is left of the century

party treats for the desperate

does fortune avoid you?
is the ship of your dreams sinking?
there is nothing to worry about
this city loves you
in barter centres boredom is stimulated
for only two bottle tops and a peso
nothing is very serious
to bear the burden of the bread and duster
only words
party treats for the desperate
for two bottle tops and a pound of meat
you get this cage
the crown of the king and a plastic sceptre
for three pounds of meat plus two degrees of fever
the swindle of insomnia
mulling over sensual nights
it loves you enormously
in barter centres
for an indiscretion plus an improper kiss
four children a dog and a chronic ulcer
nothing is very serious
life is a local matter
from work to bed
line the coffin with the silent wages of failure
moments when it rains
over the cold silk of memory
the city flooded with a stale sorrow
but how it loves you
it protects you
for two pounds of blood plus the fury
you are given three aspirins and a bullet

–Translations by **Ema Coll**

María del Carmen Colombo

María del Carmen Colombo was born in Buenos Aires in 1950. She studied Literature and Philosophy at the National University of Buenos Aires (UBA). She has published several books: *La edad necesaria* (1979); *Blues del amasijo* (1985); *Blues del amasijo y otros poemas* (1992; republished in 1998); *La muda encarnación* (1993); and *La familia china* (1999). Among other prizes, she has been awarded the Primer Gran Premio de Poesía V Centenario in 1992. Her poems have been translated into French, English, Italian and Portuguese.

Gardel and I
from *Blues del amasijo*

never
did he shout 'freckle-faced' because
I didn't have
even
one
freckle

kind
and with that
lack of imagination
he said to the camera
"I love you marilyn"

but
in those days
my name was maría
just maría

–Translated by **Esteban Moore**

María del Carmen Colombo

To See II
from *Blues del amasijo*

from the mirror
           to her body
the eyes fall like sleeping
           fruit
in her cradle of blood they will not see
where she throws the stone
      or when it will penetrate her image
or who
        (please – who)
calls her from the depth of a well

Long Tall Sally

ash feline
in the swaying skin
of dishevelled lips
         her buttocks
        moan
         in the make up
bittersweet breasts
she messes up her sorrow
        a thousand pieces
in front of the mirror
        liz
the redhead will rock and roll
some dress of glazed paper
and her eyelashes of hairy sex
that woman about
        to fly

–Translations by **Esteban Moore**

Laura Klein

Laura Klein was born in Buenos Aires in 1958. Her published works are : *A mano alzada* (1983); *Vida interior de la discordia* (1995), winner of the Boris Vian Prize; *Bastardos del pensamiento* (1997); *Del erotismo sagrado a la sexualidad científica*, in *Psicoanálisis y Género*, (2000).

with one slap

with one slap they wipe out
heads of endings or blank hands
it's all the same
they are to be feared in the solitary park
when the still one stalks strange
when they push ladies into the sea

calm down, country and you who dance
pretend to be servants: nobody
had anything nor spoke up nobody
lowered their eyes without parody
nor was there a single gesture in the light

they raise their fists and never is it the case
they have a belief they become bigger and not
worthy to sleep like an animal

on the children they tread in fury

they dress in silver or fuzz

they are to be feared when

they push ladies into the sea.

–Translated by **Beatriz Ventura**

Ana V. Lovell

Ana V. Lovell was born in Buenos Aires in 1956. She is a Professor of Literature, and has published the following books of poetry: *De cobre y barro* (1981), *Máscaras de familia* (1991) and *Jardines cerrados al público* (1999). Her poems have been translated into French.

Another Name

She who could neither build
her house with stones
nor estimate the speed of the wind
she who only doodled
symbols in the sand
drew a circle
and told herself: here is my kingdom

another name that deserves only
to be writ in water.

Like Fake Hair

Like fake hair
to the simple touch
and that sticky sensation
through the fingers
as if you had penetrated
the vagina of the world
what will you do now
with this little nothing groaning

Ceremonial

Nausea the act of fingers in the throat convulsions
Evening ritual sluicegate that opens at midnight
When the other has been walled up everybody loses their smell
in this place nobody knows how to recognize a corpse

Considerations of the corpse. Decomposition of forms.
Remains of epidermis. The depth of the water watches
The same face that lies in wait at the edge.

–Translations by **Ema Coll**

Mónica Sifrim

Mónica Sifrim was born in Buenos Aires in 1958. Her books of poetry are *Con menos inocencia* (1978); *Novela familiar* (1990); and *Laguna Bajo la luna nueva* (1999). She is a teacher and a journalist.

Galleon
from *La Carta de Oliver*

In the hold of a sunk galleon
some brandy has been discovered
so old that when one drinks it
the soul shakes lace fans.

The gold of the Indies
now lying wrinkled in a thick web
degraded the cause of notables,
bought the heart
of more than one
poor and capricious countess.

They didn't expect
that the galleon would choose to stay
beside the avid octopuses and the fleshy coral,
while history-up-there
replaced the men who died
with men
who died.

–Translated by **Esteban Moore**

Lorna Reynolds

Bird Sheltering

i.m. Claudia, died 4 July, 2001

Bird, in from the storm sheltering,
Go, fly freely. I release you,
My heart consenting.

Borne in on downward glide from Heaven,
You stayed a while. Now again
The open skies beckon, all human ties discarded,
Despite our grieving.

Bird, go, go.
Spread your wings.
Soar into your element, for all our lamenting.

Seamus Heaney

The Lift

Too timely spring: the hawthorn half in leaf.
Her funeral filled the road as it moved off,
The walkers four abreast, soon falling quiet.

Then came the throttle and articulated whops
Of a helicopter crossing and afterwards
Awareness of the rhythm of our footsteps,

Of open air and the life behind those words
'Open' and 'air'. I remembered her aghast,
Shaking, sweating, gathered, shrunk, wet-haired,

A beaten breath, a misting mask, the flash
Of one wild glance, like ghost surveillance
From behind a gleam of helicopter glass.

A lifetime, then the deathtime: reticence
Keeping us together when together,
All declaration deemed outspokenness.

Delicate since childhood, tough alloy
Of kindness, disapproval, and hauteur,
Living by herself, she knew the score

But took the risk at last of certain joys –
Her birdtable and jubilating birds.
The 'fashion' in her wardrobe and her tallboy –

And even pinned poems on her notice board.
In the end, though, it was weather said our say.
Reprise of griefs in summer's clearest mornings,

Child anniversaries that would bloom in May
Out of the simplest depths, the empyrean
There when the curtains opened every day...

They bore her lightly on the bier. Four women,
Four friends – she would have called them girls – stepped in
And claimed the final lift beneath the hawthorn.

Anthony Cronin

Childe Roland To The Dark Tower Came...

Author's Note: 'Childe' means simply a youth of noble birth, a young knight. Childe Roland first appears in a very old Scottish ballad in which he makes his way into the Dark Tower to rescue his sister held captive there by the King of Elfland. In Shakespeare's *King Lear*, the mad Edgar sings a song in which the line 'Childe Roland to the dark tower came' occurs without context or explanation. With these two previous incarnations in mind, Robert Browning wrote a poem in which Roland journeys through an horrendous landscape in search of the Dark Tower. When he finds it, he stands outside, puts his slughorn to his lips and blows it defiantly. We are not told what happened next.

Childe Roland to the dark tower came and climbed
The massive steps in natural trepidation.
But when the blonde beyond the blinding fountain
Asked him his name and business, his composure
Returned. He coolly showed his new ID
And obeying bored directions took the bronze
Lift to the fourteenth floor as he'd been told.
He smiled quite naturally at them while he noted
That Evil preferred its girls gaunt, doe-eyed, starving.
And thought it would be nice to get to know
The ones he met, while being quite aware
The person they responded to could never
Be himself. In the Dark Tower all tried
To be as was expected, not themselves.

So he must change, invent and synthesise,
Suppress both cynic and idealist,
And hide as well the hate that filled his days,
Which fed his hope and love and tenderness.
He could use some of what he was, with skill
Deploying only aspects of the self.
Quite possibly the anarchist, the dreamer,
Used strictly for effect, with guarded tongue,
Might easily impress, beguile or charm,
As had the 'characters' in his former life.
But, after all, what is the self? The much
Discussed, mulled over, moralised about,
True self, was even perhaps mythical,
Was, anyway, a burden from the past.

The first surprise was their delight in order,
Clipping and filing, typing, entering.
As if great things depended on exactness
In every single action. The new world
The Dark Tower was creating was destructive,
Oblivious, wasteful, with no end in view
Save further barren prodigality.
Within was category, calm and care,
The men in agonies of detail, logic,
Foresaw eventualities of every sort;
The slender fingers of the half-starved girls
Worked on with cool precision, almost gentle.
The end, in short, was stark and utter madness.
But the means used considerate and sane.

And then one day his work was noticed, he
Was taken down the corridor and through
A padded door, to lunch with evil in
An inner sanctum. And of course he loved it.
The subtle ambience of power obeyed
In silent smoothness and complicity
Is almost an aesthetic satisfaction.
But also there was something which to most
Of those he knew outside the building's precincts
Would come as a surprise. These men did not
Exude ambition, lust for aggrandisement
Like millionaires – or gangsters – in old movies.
Their gravity, their calm, their humour even,
Spoke only of the burdens that they bore.

And here where evil was supposed to rule
He even found a sort of fellow spirit,
Of all the most remarkable, whose gaze,
Contemplative, amused, but not unkind,
Rested on Roland while the new recruit
Outlined a project with fresh eagerness
Or offered findings with due diffidence.
The intelligent are always lonely, always
In search of fellows; but intelligence
In enterprise at least is not displayed
In inquisition of the heart or conscience
As in the cafés where the jealous poets,
Debarred from action, enviously dissected
Emotions, motives, purities of purpose.

His new friend spoke of the philosophy
– Or, rather, lack of it – the Dark Tower brought
To its activities. Alone among
The other power-systems on this planet
It was not tempted into ever seeking
To state or to define its ontologic
Reasons for being. It did not appeal
To the Great Dead or seek a mandate from
The Ancestors. It had no philosophic
Purpose that could be named, did not pretend
Or claim its power saved any Absolute
Or Moral Order in the Universe.
The Dark Tower knew the philosophic vacuum
In which mankind now lived and welcomed it.

Unlike the politicians on the podia
Who talked and tried to act as if they were
Able to adumbrate a common purpose
Transcending circumstance and even time,
Or the archaic power-systems still
Slowly decaying or collapsing round it.
The Tower did its work without pretence
To knowledge of man's ultimate destiny;
But was, he emphasised with almost passion,
The most important agent yet of history.
All others sought to limit and define:
The Tower alone to find and satisfy
Man's existential nature through his needs
And wishes, fantasies, desires.

And what more noble end could be than this one?
Or what more democratic than response
To every wish, expressed through mechanisms,
Invisible, infallible, unerring,
Machinery so natural that its working
Seemed but a law of nature liberated.
It fought no wars; it summoned to no flags.
Its power did not depend on sad prescription,
On moral exhortation, age-old deceits.
It used its influence only to ensure
The neutral freedom which was necessary
To let it do its work, entice mankind
To enter on its future, realise
With hypocrisy at last its actual nature.

When Roland woke at night now in his new
White decorated, minimalist pad
From which all evidences of a soul
Thrashing around amongst its discontents,
Passing enthusiasms, short-lived fits of purpose,
All the disorder of unordered life
Lived in the hope of love and revelation,
Had been removed, replaced by the quite simple
Serenity of a resolved equation,
He heard above the murmur of the traffic,
Going about his business in the darkness
A voice ask what it profited the soul to save
One's solipsistic, self-regarding soul
If one should lose the real world in that saving?

And for the first time in his life he was
Able to see the visible result
Of mental effort, speculative thought,
Theory and calculation. Once his joy
Had been in fitting thought to loving thought,
Premise to logical conclusion in
An ecstasy of clear contingency,
Now he was like an engineer who sees
The long curved line which was mere concept still,
Become a bridge, tectonic, actual,
Hold fast and bear its calculated weight.
The metaphors his world had used for thought –
Foundation, edifice, conclusion even –
Now seemed to him mere childishness, pretence.

The wants he satisfied with his new-found wealth
Were strangely theoretical, as are the wants
The rest of us are told we have. He bought
What young executives are supposed to buy,
An Audi V8 4.2 whose engine
Was capable of greater speeds than ever
Could be attained on any actual road,
Gadgets which he never had occasion
To use or which were quickly superseded
By different models; cameras, recorders:
Ways to reproduce the images
Of places he had no wish to revisit
And never called to mind, aids which destroy
True evocation, memory, the past.

Of course he had affairs. With gaunt, hard girls
Not unlike those he'd seen on the first day,
But more ambitious, possibly more able.
Nor were they like the girls he'd known
In all the sad cafés. These girls were not
The aimless waifs of that now lost existence.
They shared the Tower's *weltanschauung*, its values,
And though he didn't know that for some time
The Tower's ability to diminish, empty
And etiolate the sense of what was possible.
Even in bed, engaging in the acts
The magazines permitted, which were many,
There was this ebb of possibility,
This strange foreclosure of the human bounds.

The Dark Tower stood, the tallest of the tall,
But strangely light and immaterial,
Its surface chaste, sheer, almost featureless,
A shining object, its reflecting glass
Making it sphinx-like, answering no question.
Acquisitiveness and greed proclaimed at last
As ruling principles of mankind's being,
Without decree, alike without concern
For past or future, or eternity.
The Tower decided for humanity,
Whether some ate or starved, what crops they grew,
Whether they lived in tents of sacking by
Streams thick with sewage fringing smoky cities
Or scratched the soil in gangs on mountain slopes.

Roland delighted in its outward beauty;
Its chisel-thin, cloud-piercing, neutral form,
Unmoving against flowing fields of sky,
Now seemed to him Platonic, universal.
And also loved its inward-looking order,
The murmur of its air ducts soothing, steadying
Its calm and rational process of decision.
But it had roots as well, which stretched far under
Continents, seas and cities, reaching, gripping,
Blind, hungry, pale and white-tipped tentacles.
Engorging, pulping as they grew and fattened,
Groping for profit in their sightless searching,
Grasping the crumbling substances around,
Sucking the sweet sustenance from earth.

Fanny Howe

The Long Wrong

Satan fell behind, it was a taxi's shadow
where Man put his foot on the sidewalk

His mouth covered mine and he was gone

Italo once said a kiss on the mouth is the sign of betrayal
and pointed at Judas in the painting

(his muscular hand, his brush)

There was an ache in the canvas he had speared himself

That was the day when rain fell until twelve
outside the studio and twelve months before that shadow

*

Not a rink but ashed over ice
Rain on a windshield, a green light

Apartments made of dirt, neon
hangers outlined in the cleaner's window

I think proximity is the abyss
between God and us because

every fabric of my body is trying
to know why saying

I love you
in a time of extremity is a necessity

*

Dreams before waking are eyes into the future
where there is no Zurich but an alphabet

beginning with Z
so go away before I ask to know

what you mean about wanting to go

Terrified of being first?
of being dirt?

Of being ambushed or embossed? Personally
I want to batter my way out of this cage of psychology

and get to the longing I really know about

*

Morning dusk – his figure furry

Threads of gray hair

and outside, a world without a leader
Oil and landmines

Lonely words scurrying to work

If the dark bricks hide criminal life
so does each body

dedicated to maintaining power
by suppressing its delights

*

Inside this egg the walls are lacquered blue

Creamy tones of windowsill
and slat. Dawn from hell on up

I hear a rooster deny, deny, deny
or is it Man

Lies smell in every detail
as the light increases in this shell

Maybe the end of the world happened long ago
A whirl as quick as Judas breaking his neck
and every sound is an echo

*

Poor love in the order of existents

subsists on passivity inside this skin
where pain has cut a pattern

and a red heart's a little devil
speared by its own hand

and the brain of this stranger –
is it mine or its own – and its skeleton?

Can I toss them aside
like an armful of sticks and set out as a feeling
to find Hana and Issa across the night

*

Happiness has become unbearable
so don't stay with me

Ilona said this from the hall

Doors are here for both ways of walking

The split bed and bodies facing
where two unanimities
make a positive zero

She was hoping to die into Hans
so I left her house

*

I thought I was happy and said to my friend

It's because we are together

The blushing hills were rusty
its nerves as icy as his sleeves

Doll's hair, snow like artificial
Elimination of detail, a day to be grateful

He had broken parole

With speed-thinning strides
a horse passed by without a saddle

*

A body never forgets
The lens is turned on its own tremendum

Only blocks away – tubes, needles, straps
at the physician's prison

No sign of reflection, just blood and bone
trying to incorporate meds into atoms

When the body escapes without identification
this is its identification:

Chunks of moonstone smoothing a curb
Honey night snow in the city

*

She swept up my hair from the linoleum floor
and shook out the sheet

A rouge along the shades and drinks to be drunk

In transit, in transit, in stations and camps
little white spots wobbled from wall to phone

Star-lashes batted

– it was truck lights exiting the pike
and other war-zones

*

Farther wars report on us:

an arsenal of art-works and theories
that contribute to the power of the military

'Beware of the fruits of your labour!'

My father was a soldier
who was smaller than my son

when he returned as a ghost.

I begged him to stay with us
but he said: 'Not until you come to life.'

Franz Fassbind

Smog

O time of pitchblack shrouds of fume;
Caliban has defeated Ariel.

Poisonous exhalations drifting about
over meadows of harm.

The sky is a sewer;
in the lungs, the echo of greasy snow.

No glowing coals crown the days defunct.
Where the wood dies, desert grows.

By radio the last evergreens.

Notice-Serving

We do no know the soul's proportion
and disproportion.
It no longer fits
anywhere within us.

Many evict
the liberal lodger:

day after day she has
come home at late hours
(we say),
disturbed those sleeping,
and with the appeal of her clear laughter
jeopardised our reputation
(we say),
the good name of our house.

This is now vacant.

Franz Fassbind

February 21, 1948

Encircle truth
as a likely prey,
but do not fall upon her:
what use is a dead truth?

Let her live.
Leave enough room around her
and between the lines.
Room where any time,
if it suits her and
it doesn't suit you,
she can vanish.
For that, too, I think is part of truth:
that suddenly she vanishes
and returns,
and when it suits her and
it doesn't suit you.

Eclipse

A bird ploughs
the Upanishads.
With its antlers
it breaks up the crust of lies.

The true wishes of both
the living and the dead
come out finally
into the open.

Franz Fassbind

Domination

Under the
sky's glass shard,
an eagle.

Its flight is bold;
straight always in its zigzag,
it leaves no track behind.

In this setting
aimless to worry over
Prometheus's hacked liver:
it regrows.

Victims don't die out.

'Here's How I Got Out'

Who gave the
decisive
pushes,

you learn
at the earliest
after closure:

your longest
and surely your last
evening leisure.

You could finally
write the enlightening
foreword to your life.

'Take it to heart.'

–Translations from the German by **Luis Huerga**

David Lloyd

II Quartets

I.i

                quick
scattered

    these tiny beads

across the floor

how to gather them

    into the liquid bulb

where measure

    stems

I.ii

it is not

    true

the plumb lies

    unused

to this plane

    swings

       & is still

I.iii

holding to hurt

    and thrown out of yourself

as a net

    cast blindly

against the spray

I.iv

they come on

    one by one

cresting

to fix one

    like a cite

and it breaks

        shingles

II.i

      The story is shy

trailing

    across the skyface

failing through the lightgates

    its gravitas

sleeps through my fingers

utter
              precipitate

           breath sore

            in the gullet

II.ii

The free zone (space

    contracts:

      a room

        a niche

      a coign

of vantage

music from the back room

    (she plays on

fingers wedged in the crevice

    breeze tuned

II.iii

out of words

back there

yawn yourself

 into the cloudscape

dark with night rips

the wind tears in

nothing

the clearing

the cleaving

II.iv

relief

   (as in bas relief

     an exhalation

thrown into relief

   against the skyline

(the lightness of ash

   lifting in the hearth

that tower with the shattered step

   abrupt

        brink

        stone

        ateeter

Denise Blake

The Field of Bones (translation of *Gort na gCnámh* by Cathal Ó Searcaigh)

1

Girl, the light is fading, he barks
    out of nowhere
as if I had the slightest control
    over the night.
Oh, Christ, if that churlish fool
    only understood
half of what he said. My father, the thran
    brutal bastard.
I'm trailing the track of his spade
    with heavy steps;
a snivelling, tattered mess. Hoking out spuds
    in a savage wind.
Was I always like this? My memories
    are tainted, putrid.
He breaks the soil's thick skin
    with ease,
presses on stubbornly. Digging ahead of him,
    all turned behind him.
Such an unforgiving place, without shelter
    from gales or storms.
I sacrificed myself to this earth;
    my sweat softened the clay,
the tears made it fertile
    and still it demands more.

2

I lost it all, here, in the Field of Bones.
    My hope was buried
in this earth. He always said, *There's good bone*
    in this ground,
as he rubbed the soil with the claws
    of the Devil.
The Field of Bones I named this awful

      bog-land
when only a slip of a girl. Wasn't I right?
I gave it my flesh. I gave it my blood.
      I gave it my baby.
Now I'm destroyed. The prospective plains
      of my mind
have turned to a weed-tangled wilderness.
I carry the shape of an old hag
      or a stump of dried bog-wood
in the frozen wastelands of winter.
      I am ugly.
Depression nightmares me
through the daylight, through the twilight,
      in eternal shadows.
Darkness a thousand times worse,
a thousand times denser,
      than the blackness
of the final floods from the barren hills of
      Keeldrum.

3

It was his sin. He came between me
      and night's sweet sleep;
between me and God's mercy – if I ever believed
      in God's mercy.
I was only thirteen when he shattered
      his duty of care
and jumped into my bed. A night in early spring
      just six weeks
after my Mother's passing. But, I tell you,
she has no fault, the creature hadn't the strength
      for her life.
I ll knock the Sunday girl out of you,
      you useless whore;
as he lifted his fist, knocked her through the house.
      He crushed her heart.

Turned her into a shambling mute.
    Consumption – how are you –
sent her to the grave in her forties.
    We were left,
himself and myself, in a cold stone cottage,
    for I was their only child.
He slithered towards me under the cover of night.
    Greasy, naked flesh.
Daddy, what are you doing? Daddy?
    I was half-asleep
as he tore my blue flowered nightdress off me.

4

Then he was on top of me like an old hound,
    slobbering and pawing.
Mangy chest hairs stuck in my mouth.
    He jammed into me,
ripping my insides with his thick runt
    until he howled.
He pulled away. I lay heaped.
    Too frightened to cry.
Stared out at the stars sparkling
as the candles at my Mother's wake.
And so he came at me, at any hour.
    Horror throbbing in his breeches.
He carried me off like a sack of spuds
    to the manure filled byre;
or pinned me there, by the bramble hedge,
    or here, in the Field of Bones.
Scattered his seed in the clay of my womb.
    I was his hostage.
At seventeen I was carrying a child
    conceived by a curse,
and shame wouldn't tell my tale.
Did the townies think my sudden weight,
was me following my people's plump nature
    – or did they take any heed?

5

By the end of autumn, caught in the waves
    of labour.
I came here to give birth,
    to a child with no welcome
as the wind screeched over Maladuff.
    I had a daughter.
My mid-wife was an old dog bitch,
who lapped up my blood, chewed on afterbirth.
    And while stars burned,
reddened like hayricks blazing on the sky's
shorn pastures, I held the tiny harvest
    of my womb.
    Held her safe.
Before my murderous fingers finished her.
Nothing could strangle the scream
    I gave to that night.
I buried her there, in the soil between a hawthorn
    and the granite stones.
I stayed here. How could I bear the world,
    if I couldn't bear myself?
Nothing faced me but savage grief,
forever bogged in the quagmire of Seasceann.

6

Where could I go – this girl who never travelled
    past Letterkenny.
I hadn't the courage, I hadn't the wit,
    to up and leave.
Couldn't place a penny in my palm.
    Everywhere held distress for me.
My light was smothered. Hope tangled
    on barbed briers.
And now I've spent twenty-five years, swinging
from manic frenzy to deathly inertia.
    Twenty-five years.
Never once did a local lad think
    to come courting –

let alone come for my hand.
A good man could have freed me
    from all this wretchedness.
I threw a slew of curses at my father.
Brandished the black-handled knife
    kept scabbard by my side;
    sharpened by my hatred.
I have him warned, if he ever touches me
he will not escape with his life.
    We have no contact,
will never have contact, even past our end.

7

I can see sparkles of home lights;
Fanaboy, Keedrom, Cashelnagcorr,
    beacons of warmth
as loneliness freezes my heart.
I keep gathering from drill to drill
    down and up, down and up,
following the metronome of the spade.
    I feel heavy,
wearing a weight of grief and guilt,
    an unrelenting burden.
I know my courage would grow
    if I could give birth
to the pressure conceived in my mind,
bring my thoughts forth safely.
    When I try,
when I open my mouth for that voice,
my throat ensnares the words.
    They become rigid
and a lifeless stillbirth falls from me.
    Once again there is a burial
between hawthorn and granite stones.
    No cross for the resting
as a black crow caws and a lone robin
    remains silent.
This is the dirge Mother Fate
    wants for me.

Randolph Healy

Storms

The reason my sister was screaming
was that the cloth I had grabbed
and used to mop up spilt black tea
was our mother's unshakeable favourite.
There was no going back.
I hid it in the shed.
That evening, in an unannounced first
my mother went out herself to get the coal
and returned to swat me around the front room
with the carbonned tanninned tea-cloth
of enormous sentimental value.
There was anger
glittering and transient
as the colours in a just caught fish.
Her last wish was that her ashes
be brought back to Ardrossan.
The ground is full of famous men.

Randolph Healy

Primula Veris

Clustering atop a leggy stem
ten elf green bodices tapered down
to blown about yellow pinafores.

Near the ground a mob of blotched leaves,
belching and gulping, stiff with liquor,
watched constellations kink and bend
and languages drift from grammar to grammar.

Sister Mary's favourite flower
cast a light on all the goudgers
that she coaxed, effing and blinding,
to various degrees of joined-up writing.

One great arching cadence
glosses the world as a double spiral
speaks to itself with epochs for clauses

root shoot and flower
stitching together the heavens and the earth.

Eamon Grennan

On Achill

Deep as it might be, what is our silence to the silence of the
village of Slievemore, its upstanding skeleton stones open to the
blows any weather off the ocean can throw, its grassed lanes and
main street given over to the air since hunger struck and laid
them low, hunting the shawled and barefoot villagers onto the
roads towards the boats at Louisburgh and the long haul to
Newfoundland or South Boston, their old home a haven now for
gulls, a hawk or two, or cormorants crashing down among the
grey rocks to weather and sit out the storm's ferocity? And what
is the slight edgy freeze that folded snow and cliffs of ice over
most of the island, though it left a corner of it free to be itself –
so strange shapes of land and stranger flowers settled there,
surprising visitors.

A Death

Light as a feather the way he slipped away: nothing
of Oedipus in it, no thunderclaps of applause
as the old man goes off-stage into mystery. It is
the silence after, though, that has to be the same:

slipping into everything, lying between one nature
and the next, or falling like it fell last night at dinner
when the three of us in a lull of talk put our elbows
on the table and sat watching the candle flicker a little
in the cross-currents of our breath, one breath coming
after another in silence, like that, light as a feather.

Maurice Scully

Three pages from 'Broken Ceremony'

...the money I can see
    from here
landing on the floor
    emitting little words
is not for me
    [where's my home?
how house
    my children?]
& when the breezes shake
    the leaves a little
they all fall over
    into another country
evenly speaking
    Utopian-Glass-Box.
oh I'll be there –
    mouth wide –
interpreting off-key...

    then I woke up.

moving from the small
    stinking hotel
arranged for us by
    the school & too
expensive anyway
    to what turned out
to be some sort of
    brothel & then on
a few days later
    on his insistence
to a colleague's place.
    & his collapsing
marriage.
    drunkenness. fights.
a television
    flung to the floor.

we'd arrived – yes –
  but not quite yet
to that distant spot of
  sunlight where to
disport our wings over
  the forest floor.

... space – air –
scattering influence
  over us – a
matter of discussion –

  doubt + idiocy
join the club –
  a split stone
in the storm/
  black white/
it glints & (click)
  purrs (of) yr
properties' keys
  in my pockets
index of what you
  think & what you think is
yours by right – not
  omitting that niggling
ever-present fever
  to survive –
rain of dishonest
  badgerings
incessant valley
  of darkness –
it dissolves
  love blurs
at the edges
  gestelted thalurbs
overolve in the
  deep blue sea (will
I begin it?) the world.
  (that's all that's in it:

blue veins / pink
    vines) then what?
gis a job – & so –
    down. (*earth*)
                that.
land on it.
    ignition –
back to the crannóg
    for me...

the angle of
the neck the
angle of the
bill the angle

& elevation of
the body the
ruffling of the
feathers on the

back & the di
    splay of
    the tail.

    pipe
        pip
    curl
        rill.

    swirl
        sculpt
    split.

do-fheicithe
    in braille...

Michael Smith

Poet of Reality and Desire: Luis Cernuda (1902-1963)

Although unjustly less well known outside Spain than the work of other members of the famous Generation of '27, the poetry of Luis Cernuda is very highly regarded in the hispanic world, and tributes are already appearing in great numbers this year to mark the centenary of his birth.

Luis Cernuda was born in Seville in 1902, and had two sisters. The domestic ambience was traditional and claustrophobically restrictive. Cernuda's homosexuality seems to have manifested itself early in his life, even if not clearly to Cernuda himself until he was about fourteen. Confusion about his sexual orientation was a major cause of his introversion, and his early life, in particular his teens, seems to have been lonely and even tormented.

At the University of Seville, Cernuda began the study of Law. There he met Pedro Salinas and, while attending his courses in Spanish Language and Literature, became friendly with him. Salinas encouraged his literary efforts, invited him to his home and introduced him to modern French poetry. Later, the reading of Gide would have a profound influence on Cernuda, helping reconcile him to his homosexuality.

Although his father died in 1920, Cernuda continued his university studies for two more years, without distinction. From 1920 to 1924 he did his military service, and then began writing the short poems of his first book, *Perfil del Aire* ('Profile of the Air'). He came to know Juan Ramón Jiménez, and established relationships with Lorca and Aleixandre. Also around this time he became a dandy, dressing with ostentatious finesse.

On the death of his mother in 1928, Cernuda abandoned his native Seville, sold the family house and, assisted by Salinas, obtained a lectureship in Spanish Language and Literature in the University of Toulouse. But in 1929 he returned to Madrid and found employment in a bookshop.

In 1934 he collaborated in left-wing journals. This marks

Cernuda's short-lived political engagement during which he became a member of the Communist Party. He travelled throughout Spain on behalf of the Republican Government, giving lectures and writing for *Heraldo de Madrid*.

In 1935 he discovered the poetry of Hölderlin and, with help, managed to read the great German in the original and even to translate some of his poems. In the following year all the poetry which Cernuda had written up till then was collected in the book *La Realidad y el Deseo* ('Reality and Desire') which was to become the common title of all his poetry. On the occasion of this publication, Lorca dedicated an *homenaje* to Cernuda which was attended by the most important members of the Generation of '27. This ended the first phase of Cernuda's career; the next is that of exile without return, *exilio sin vuelta*.

In 1936 Cernuda went to Paris as secretary to the Spanish Ambassador there. Later in the same year, however, he returned to Madrid until the eruption of the Civil War, when he moved to Valencia. There, with other poets, he established the magazine *Hora de España*. In February of 1938 he left again for Paris, and from there made his way to England on the pretext of giving some lectures. Cernuda would never return to Spain.

Cernuda stayed in Britain until 1947, and then took up a teaching position in Massachusets, where he made a relatively good living. Then, in 1949, he visited Mexico for the first time, and immediately fell in love with the people and the country (reminding him of his native Seville). Every summer he holidayed in Mexico, and there, in 1951, when Cernuda was 49, he fell in love with a young man, and in the first great outburst of erotic love wrote *Poemas para un cuerpo* ('Poems for a body'). In 1952 he decided to live in Mexico permanently.

Financially pressed, Cernuda returned to the United States in 1960 as a teacher and lecturer, this time in Los Angeles. In 1963 he returned finally to Mexico, embittered, disillusioned and alone – as indeed he mostly had been throughout his adult life. He died suddenly in the same year.

His poetry is unabashedly direct. In a sense, almost all of it can be read as a soliloquy, even when the speaker seems to be addressing others. Maniacally self-absorbed, Cernuda wrote to discover, to justify and to console himself. He derived some consolation from the beauty of the natural world and from music and painting. A profoundly alienated character, both socially and even from his own body, he was haunted by the image of a lost childhood paradise, a paradise from which he was cast out by his sexual orientation and his withdrawn personality. The moments of epiphanic transcendence which occur in his poems are of reunion with a whole, uninhibited self.

All in all, Cernuda was a man ill-at-ease with the world in which he found himself. His prickly aloofness and irascibility shielded an acute sense of his own vulnerability. He was not, by all accounts, a very lovable man. No doubt his upbringing explains much, as may his tormented sexuality. But, read less reductively, his poetry speaks poignantly of the loneliness of the human condition, and it offers the reader a deeply human, if painfully frank, companionship.

Luis Cernuda

Ancient Garden

To go again to the sealed garden
that hides, behind a mud wall
and arches, among magnolias,
lemon trees, its waters' charm.

To hear again in the silence,
alive with birdsong and leaves,
the cool sighing of the wind
where old souls are floating.

To see again faraway
the deep sky, the slender tower,
such a flower of light on the palms:
all things always beautiful.

To feel again, as then,
the sharp thorn of desire,
while past youth
returns. Dream of a timeless god.

–Translated by **Michael Smith**

Tony Frazer

Letter from London

Reading through major poetry-related journals from the UK can be an odd experience. Journals and magazines such as *Poetry Review*, *PN Review* and the like take their subject very seriously, and imply that it is of significant import. The reality, in the greater scheme of things, is that poetry is almost invisible on the greater literary landscape bar the occasional effusion from the Poet Laureate – such as when aged members of the Royal family pass away – and the occasional piece in the broadsheet press when a poet has been placed 'in-residency' somewhere unusual, such as a bank or a lawyer's office. Contemporary poetry is treated as a Cinderella product beloved of an odd coterie of devotees that the larger world regards as being on a level similar to committed conservationists, unreconstructed socialists and so forth: worthy persons all, but given to odd clothing and even odder statements. The fact is that poetry has almost ceased to be the subject of comment amongst the lettered classes, and every announcement of its revival is little more than a publicity stunt above a mouldering corpse.

For myself I must plead guilty to being one of the oddballs toiling in the shadows; I edit a little magazine, of small but pleasing reputation, devoted almost entirely to contemporary poetry, and a small press (ditto). These ventures receive no subsidy (nor am I sure that they deserve it – I have never sought it — but more of that later), and struggle to get heard in a literary marketplace that actually has little regard in general for poetry that is not simple on the surface and instantly communicative. I am often guilty of printing work that normal literate readers find puzzling, closed, abstract, difficult etc. Poetry alas is classified simply as 'poetry'. It is not hyphenated in any way or permitted to be sub-classified by genre in the way that fiction is, which is probably to its detriment, although there was a time when there were pop-poets, and there are now some performance-poets on the scene. Most readers are aware that there are experimental or 'avant-garde' poets, but further sub-classification of the field would be beyond even the most observant commentators. This probably accounts for the large number of letters I receive from innocent would-be contributors, who announce that they have written a Poem (always capitalized), which they would be prepared to permit me to publish. It is a curious fact that the world seems to be full of writers of poetry, but empty of readers of it, if one is to judge by the sales figures of even those publishing houses regarded as specialists in the field. It is such simple and awkward facts that lead to sneering comments that "poets only write for each other": alas, there is a grain of truth in the jibe. The error is that the fact arises not from intention on the writer's part. Why can we not be honest and admit that Wendy Cope is not the same kind of poet as, say, Paul Muldoon, even if they do share a publisher? Light classical music is filed separately in the CD racks; romantic fiction gets its own section in the bookstore, but in poetry they're all Poets, be they Patience Strong or Sappho. We don't position our product very well, I suspect.

The dominant mode in contemporary English poetry (less so in Scottish and Welsh writing) is very much in the post-Movement style: relentlessly demotic and downbeat. Often very clever, despite limited use of the language's resources, modern English poetry can however be depressingly unambitious, even when making claims to ambition. Tom Paulin's latest, *The Invasion Handbook*, is a case in point: a poetic history of the Second World War overwhelmed by its scope and background research, and dominated by a slack a-rhythmic verse line that drifts into near-prose. It is a sign of the times that books such as this and Anne Carson's *The Beauty of the Husband* receive respectful reviews that concentrate on the content and ignore the writer's handling of the medium. (Ms Carson is Canadian, and thus *hors de combat* here, but she has recently won the T S Eliot Prize for this particular book.) For the record, *The Beauty of the Husband*, a book that I rather enjoyed reading, should probably be read as an experimental prose work, despite its being chopped into left-adjusted lines. When a really knotty piece of fine poetic writing does come along, such as in Geoffrey Hill's two most recent volumes (*Speech! Speech!* and *The Orchards of Syon* – though the latter is as yet only available in the USA), the response is all too often a condescending sniff, accompanied by mutterings that the writer is 'Not Quite Our Sort.' Intellectuals are not wanted here apparently, above all not those whose political and social views might be described as High Anglican. Hill's mortal sin is probably that he lives in Boston. Thom Gunn in San Francisco, Christopher Middleton in Austin, and Nathaniel Tarn in Santa Fe are likewise often looked at askance, in common with many of their American brethren, perhaps because their broader horizons threaten the relentlessly restrained local status quo. So far this has not affected Paul Muldoon in Boston, but he is a more recent emigrant. And if Hill should be regarded with suspicion, with his track record, imagine what the responses are to J H Prynne, doyen of the poetic avant-garde.

While the official centre takes refuge in little-Englandism, the avant-garde (or the innovative poets, or the experimental poets, or the little pressers, or whatever one wishes to call them) occupies a nether world parallel to the apparent mainstream. The two sides rarely read each other, often on principle, but the disagreements are rarely heard in public as the two sides do not meet, let alone speak. When, inadvertently, they do meet, misunderstandings inevitably occur. Last year the much-garlanded Sean O'Brien tried to enter into a debate with some members of an e-mail-based discussion group devoted to contemporary poetry (of an avant-garde persuasion), and ended up withdrawing under a torrent of abuse. The prelude to his withdrawal was the inability of either O'Brien or his interlocutors to agree on the terms of the discourse. Even the basic words – influence, mainstream, etc. – meant different things to different people. Later in 2001, O'Brien then reviewed a new anthology of British and Irish poetry[1] from the USA in flagrantly insulting and unprofessional terms. The anger was palpable, and hopefully did not simply arise from the author's own exclusion from the selection in question, for the abuse he heaped upon this excellent volume was directed almost entirely at the latter pages, where the chosen poets are split almost exactly 50/50 between the mainstream and avant-garde camps of contemporary British and Irish verse. O'Brien objected also to some older work, chiefly that of certain forgotten modernists from between the wars, and in one or two cases there, I would agree with him. At no point did his argument proceed from an identifiable aesthetic position, however, an unfortunate trait that he shares with some of his avant-garde enemies. The sad thing about this was that the torrent of abuse appeared in *Poetry Review*, organ of the Poetry Society of Great Britain and would-be arbiter of taste in contemporary British verse. A chance was thus lost to initiate a debate in a place, which should, by its very nature, be hosting it. I do not for one moment begrudge Sean O'Brien his opinions. The world would after all be a much poorer place if we all agreed with one another all the time, but it would have been better to engage with the work he disliked (which constituted no more than 20% of the book) and attempt to explain to the readership what was going on. Of course the poor fellow might have had a problem understanding the poetry of, say, John Wilkinson – most of us do, I suspect – but it is the

[1]Keith Tuma (ed.): *Anthology of Twentieth-Century British and Irish Poetry* (Oxford University Press, New York, 2001)

reviewer's task to engage, not abdicate and rant. Nonetheless, whatever my own views here, the little ghetto of English mainstream verse is likely to repel boarders who appear to threaten the edifice in which they dwell. 'Twas ever thus.

*

At a recent gathering of those who like the kind of poetry I publish and follow – the Cambridge Conference on Contemporary Poetry, initials deliberately thus – I made one of those serendipitous acquaintances on the first evening. I had been talking to an interesting fellow, slightly older than I, but had not registered his name. After a while some kind person said, "Tony, do you know Richard Burns?" indicating my interlocutor. At which point I said, "Richard Burns, the poet?", a question which was greeted with a raised eyebrow and admission of culpability. Now, I had at that time four volumes of Richard Burns' verse on my shelves, all of which I had found of great interest. One in particular, the early *Avebury*, very much a work of its time (late 1960s / early 1970s), remains to this day a favourite long poem. I had only recently come across the fourth volume, a selected poems from the mid-90s, put out by an unknown (to me) publishing house in Norwich. This book proved that Burns was still active and still doing very interesting things, even if the editor had committed the cardinal error of not including anything from *Avebury*. I had found this book six months previously, and completely by accident, on the shelves of Borders in London's Charing Cross Road – yes, on the shelves of an international-chain bookstore, whose selection was otherwise the predictable collection of Faber poets and A-level set texts. How this single copy got there I shall never know, but I'm happy I found it. Since this meeting, I've learned that Burns has just published a long poem – 150 pages long, and in 100 sections – called *The Manager*. This, to compound the previous discovery, is also published by an outfit I've never heard of, Elliott and Humphries of London, and very handsome it is too. From a poetry point of view this book is far more interesting than the prize-winning Anne Carson book mentioned above, but Burns lacks the cachet of the Canadian and thus also lacks the profuse level of admiration accorded the younger poet. It's a shame, but I suspect that Burns' work will be remembered longer than Carson's.

*

Serendipity can strike in other ways: this week it was via my mailbox. Just a month ago I had been trying to track down the excellent American poet Roberto Tejada, some years ago editor of the wonderful bilingual (Spanish/English) magazine *Mandorla*. I had been foolish enough to lose contact with him during my own wanderings, and tried e-mailing his last known e-address. No response, but no electronic rejection either. Then, three days ago a package of books arrived from New Haven, CT., including one by, yes, Roberto Tejada. The covering letter from the publisher, Phylum Press, was even more interesting. Apparently Tejada had asked them to send it to me, so maybe that message did get through after all, but they decided to add in two more chapbooks because they admired a book I had published last year by the expatriate American poet Karin Lessing. A very nice gesture in itself, but more interesting yet was Phylum's modus operandi. None of their chapbooks are sold; they are given away to deserving persons suggested by the author and the editors. Production seems to occur when there's enough spare cash to meet the printing bill. Each chapbook is hand-stitched and individually finished, and in some cases artists design them; the Tejada volume has sewing machine stitches across the cover and a plastic zipper.

The other volumes were by Peter Gizzi – serendipity again, as I'd met him last year when he visited Exeter – and Cathy Eisenhower. Now I don't know Ms Eisenhower, but the book is based on her experiences of life in Chile – where I also lived for a couple of years in the early 90s. I suspect my quota of chance encounters and serendipity has been used up for the year, but I hope not.

Phylum's approach is self-consciously anti-capitalist, and is in many ways admirable. These are people who believe in what they're doing and take it to its logical extreme. It's an interesting response to the distribution issue affecting poetry: the fact that most bookstores that carry poetry in the UK are chain stores whose rationale is of course to move the maximum number books per square foot of retail space. This is quite understandable, alas. These stores – located conveniently in expensive real estate – have massive fixed overheads to cover, large numbers of staff, and shareholders who naturally want a return on their investment. Poetry, with its low sales, cannot figure too prominently in such an environment and it's foolish to expect it to do so, but some of these stores, when managed by a sympathetic individual, will host literary events out of hours and provide a little space for local writers. If you're looking to browse though, you won't be in luck, as Ed Foster recently discovered. Foster is the editor of *Talisman* magazine and the Talisman House press in New Jersey, and recently visited London. (The magazine is, in my view, one of the best in the USA at present, and the press has a record of putting out excellent books, including two eye-opening anthologies[2] which prove that there is a vibrant tradition of groundbreaking poetry which avoids academic formalism on the one hand and the ludicrous non-referential 'language' poetry on the other. Those books were a relief.) Now on his trip to London, Foster thought he would browse the bookstores, and, to his stunned surprise, he found not one, not a single one, that carried a literary journal of any kind. He was of course looking in the wrong place, and was doubly depressed to discover that the old standby, Compendium Books in Camden Town, had closed its doors after more than three decades.

My response to this was that one has to know where to look, but that there isn't much there anyway. We are in fact in a transitional phase, I think, in which poetry is becoming a disintermediated product. Until recently the path for any book was writer-publisher-bookstore-reader, sometimes with an editor or an agent along the way. It is now moving towards a writer-publisher-reader path or even writer-reader, with the Internet, the great enabler, as the distribution mechanism. I see books becoming prestige objects, with prices to match, although the advent of efficient print-on-demand technologies may well stave this off. My own magazine has just begun to gravitate to the internet, so far as an adjunct to the printed version, but I do wonder how long I will be able to keep them going in tandem. Another possibility, suitable only for a large city, is a subvented store dedicated to marginal interests. There is a model for this in Germany, where the *Autorenbuchhandlung* (literally *Authors' Bookshop*) has three branches, in Berlin, Frankfurt and Munich. It was started in Berlin in the 50s by Günter Grass and some friends, who thought it necessary to have an outlet for poetry, drama and contemporary arts that regular bookstores could or would not stock. Each branch, but especially the one in Berlin, is a treasure-trove for anyone like myself who has a fascination with contemporary German poetry. All the small presses are there, all the journals that are really looking for an audience. Readings occur on the premises, and there's a splendid bar just next door to which you can adjourn when it all gets too thirsty. Oh for a Maecenas in London, or perhaps in Edinburgh or Dublin, who would start such a venture and ensure that knowledgeable staff are employed and paid a decent rate. Daydreaming again.

---

[2]*Primary Trouble: An Anthology of Contemporary American Poetry*, edited by Schwartz, Donahue and Foster (1996), and *An Anthology of New (American) Poets*, edited by Jarnot, Schwartz and Stroffolino (1998)

Randolph Healy

The Wandering Wood

A poem can be anything. *What will you not be sniffing?*[1] As I write this our three-year-old, Beatrice, is coming back from our hen-house with a single egg in her hand. Miraculously, it arrives unbroken, a feat which robots find surprisingly difficult to emulate. Never mind the uneven terrain, egg after egg is dropped or crushed as they under- or over-estimate the degree of strength required to hold them. Beatrice's solution is to keep the egg on the point of falling, continually releasing her grip until micro-slips between the shell and the whorls of her fingertips cue her to tighten her hold infinitesimally, the process, as is typical of living things, permeable to information flowing in both directions.

A fool sees not the same tree that the wise man sees.[2] While she would more likely prefer the rôle of the tree to either the other two parts, I can hardly guess what Bea sees as she picks her way past the hawthorns, down the slope back to our house. For a long time I found the fact of empathy, or even basic conversation difficult to account for. I had been working for some years with a pocket calculator (computers were way out of my financial reach at that stage) trying, on the one hand, to bring my intuitive and intellectual accounts of the world closer together, and on the other to put myself in the position of having new (to me) intuitions. *There are more stars in the universe / than all the words ever spoken, / as many stars as atoms in a matchstick.*[3] Yet, though the edges of our universe are expanding at almost the speed of light, the place is so big that, proportionally, Beatrice is growing billions of times faster. With this degree of elbow room even a planet can seem quite inconsequential. If the entire Earth disappeared in a puff of smoke, the loss of matter would be no more noticeable than if an atom fell off your body. What of the human dimension? Taking all the people who ever were, in all of history, estimated to be about a hundred billion people, the crowd wouldn't fill Leinster, a province of Ireland, itself a crumb off the Western coast of Europe. Nevertheless, I find Russell's self-description as a 'tiny lump of impure carbon and water impotently crawling on a small and unimportant planet'[4] more convincing as theatre than as philosophy. There must be some way of looking at this child so that her extraordinary nature is not erased by mere scale.

How often / in this loneliness, / unlighted... [5] My mother was born in Belfast in 1920. Her family had to move to Scotland to avoid the violence of the time, her parents' mixed marriage making them a target of both sides. My father, born three years later in a tenement in the capital of the Irish Free State, saw several of his siblings die. After his mother had a breakdown her children were taken into care. Conditions were scarcely less harsh in the orphanage to which my father was assigned (inexplicably, and heartlessly, his brothers and sister were sent to different institutions). His unremitting 'that was very tasty' after every dinner, no matter what was on the menu, used to puzzle me until I found out that he used to have to run his meal, stale bread, under a tap in the orphanage until it became possible to chew it. As soon as he was legally allowed, he left school and went to work as a messenger boy for the post office. My mother's family had settled in Scotland and were very happy here. However, with the commencement of the Second World War, she was given an ultimatum: either work in the munitions factory in Ardeer or be deported back to Northern Ireland. Not wishing to lose her family, friends and work, she stayed. It must have been an extraordinary place, a great park full of small huts about a hundred yards apart. Every now and then a hut would go up and she would have lost another friend. I don't know how she stuck it.

My mother and father were originally pen-friends. When they married, the question as to which country they would live in arose. It was not settled immediately, and for years they lived apart. In the end, after my elder sister and I were born, she reluctantly moved to Ireland. I don't think she was ever really happy there, and whenever she said home she meant Scotland.

... ourselves / So infinitesimally scaled // We could stream through the eye of a needle.[6] I liked school, and English and Mathematics in particular. Our class of 48 pupils in the primary school had, unusually, the same teacher for all six years, a kindly, well-read man, Jim O'Sullivan, from Cork. Though even he could not entirely prevail over the insular tendencies of the Irish education system. For example, I remember in 1966 we had been studying the 1916 Easter Rising for weeks. *Gold banners between houses in every town*[7]. (For the mathematically catatonic I will point out that it was the 50th anniversary of the rising, and it was celebrated in the most uncritically adoring terms everywhere. I felt a

little left out as my mother ignored it completely as something merely and contemptibly Irish, and my father hardly said a word anyway. My friends all seemed to be learning the correct feelings to have about this great event at home, while I was left all at sea.) Eventually our puzzlement swelled to the point where somebody asked the teacher why the leaders were so summarily shot. It seemed too harsh. Mr. O'Sullivan got a distant look in his eye and said, "Well, you see, there was a war in Europe at the time." This was the first hint we'd had of World War I. And we only knew about World War II because of films and the comics: 'Die *Britisher Schweinhund! Achtung! Schnell! Schnell*' and so on.

my telescope leans blind against the wall / its mirror cataracted with fresh dust[8]. About this time it was discovered that I needed glasses. But when I got them, I couldn't see a thing. So I developed the habit of looking through the gap between my nose and their metal bridge. This required some concentration and, I suspect, quite a degree of facial distortion, as my teacher and my mother asked me what was going on. I explained my difficulty. My mother, who could be quite a sport, took me at my word and made another appointment with the ophthalmologist. Said august personage refused to countenance any possibility of error and ticked me off for not wanting to wear them. My mother then brought me to a private optician who discovered a plus where a minus should have been and explained that the glasses were four times too strong for me. They must have been hummers because what I normally wear are real bottle ends. The new pair worked like a charm, and for the first time my world came into focus. I wasn't entirely sure I liked this, but at least it took the guesswork out of getting a bus.

I began secondary school and then things went a bit pear-shaped. I became ill and was bedridden a good deal of the time. My medication had side-effects which included disrupting concentration and causing memory loss to various degrees. This made reading next to impossible as I found it extremely difficult to remember what it was I had just read. In the end I left school at the age of fourteen. Having no qualifications, the range of careers open to me was limited. My first job was as a sales assistant in a jewellery shop. The shop employed two watch repairers and I found their work fascinating. By and large the days were pleasantly uneventful. Though one time I barged into the back office without knocking and disturbed the boss who was busy cracking teeth for their gold fillings. Some of the teeth appeared to have some kind of, well, flesh attached to them. Another day we heard a loud bang. My immediate reaction was that it was some kind of bomb. This turned out to be correct. The shop was closed and we started for home. There were no buses and I had to make my way on foot. I remember running down interminable faded Georgian terraces, unable to take my eye off the buildings, as if mere looking would keep them up. After a year I left this job with the idea of taking correspondence courses, but the difficulties mentioned above soon returned me to the workforce where I successively took up the roles of Hoffmann presser, telex typist, security man and housepainter. *I'd make a first-rate detective. / Except for the bits that involve courage. / and expertise. and enthusiasm for the whole thing*[9]. After four years I was able to return to school, and then attended Trinity College Dublin, where I studied Mathematical Sciences.

Logic is a mechanism / made of infinitely hard material.[10] I'd been writing poetry from the age of twelve, mainly short intense lyrics. My final year in college was a watershed in which my conception of poetry expanded considerably. The catalyst for this was the experience of hearing Maurice Scully reading ten or eleven times as part of a road-show organised by Dermot Bolger. I liked Maurice's work immediately, especially its flexible line. He suggested to me that I consider a poetry of ideas which led me to consider strategies derived from mathematical logic. In his History of Western Philosophy, Russell time and again criticises philosophers for not following an argument wherever it may lead. The scholastic philosophers are particularly scolded for their habit of bending the rules in order to 'prove' statements which their beliefs required them to hold true. He was, of course, being more than a little unfair. Still, thanks to them logic is often associated with unyielding dogmatism, duplicity even. Euclid's twelve-volume *Elements of Geometry* was their model. They believed that his geometry was a faithful transcription of reality, and that its form – using a very small number of 'self-evident' propositions and the rules of Aristotelian logic to prove or even generate a vast number of geometrical principles – would transfer to theology the irrefutability of mathematics. There was also a belief that geometry was not empirical, that its results could be deduced entirely from reason. This could be taken as a metaphor for revelation, something independent of experience. Pythagoras had attempted a similar cross breeding of religion and mathematics. Overwhelmed by his discovery that musical intervals could be described in terms of ratios of natural numbers, he decreed that all of nature was rational and that all its properties could be so expressed. Very soon it was discovered that the square root of two cannot be equal to any ratio of whole numbers. (The proof is beautiful[11]). Knowledge of this was suppressed, and violence, even murder, done to those who tried to make it public. But they couldn't keep a lid on it. Nor could the scholastic theologians prevent the discovery of non-Euclidean geometry and non-Aristotelian logic. I had no interest in logic as a machine for cranking out absolute truths or for riveting one's beliefs together. Indeed, in their failed attempt to deduce mathematics from purely logical considerations, Whitehead and Russell showed that logic was a far more interesting entity. Paradoxes[12] emerged which seemed to be woven into the very fabric of the discipline. Logical systems were later shown to be incomplete, i.e. not every proposition can be proved to be either true or false. They were shown to be incapable of proving their own consistency without the aid of a meta-system, which would in turn require its own meta-system and so on. A key idea in analytic philosophy used to be that the fundamental principles underlying reality were simple, self-evident and hence irrefutable. A sure recipe for dogma. The exotic paradoxes laid bare by modern logic, inescapable, impenetrable, insoluble, liberate the discipline from the chain theory of truth. There is no starting point. You may start where you will.

Apart from its epistemological instability, I was interested in the formal and contentual possibilities that logical form opened up. Following an argument wherever it leads can bring you to unexpected places. The sentence structure itself can allow one to be open to ideas which ordinary syntax would fail to suggest. Then again, its organising principles allow for a music of ideas, where music is not just noise (which I'm all for) but the arrangement of relationships in time. It also fostered clarity and density. If you think of me bumbling along, periodically half-blind and forgetting everything, the attraction these held will be obvious.

Within several months of all this, Maurice Scully published my first book, a chapbook called *25 Poems*. Its contents were divided between the logical pieces and the more obviously traditional memory poems. Both types have plenty of precedents in the history of poetry, Lucretius offering an obvious example. I wished to move on and the next step was to begin working on calculator poems. Aesthetically, this seemed a straightforward development, going from logic to arithmetic to science. Personally, I wished to find alternative vantage points to that offered by my frequently overwhelming personal history. The spirit behind the project was one of expansion, not erasure.

> they bounce back from the screen
> clean and ready
> making parts of the body
> an aesthetic obligation
> before the skeleton bursts out[13]

The first entry in the large spiral-bound notebook I kept for the next eight years concerned the masses, diameters and thicknesses of the various Irish coins. This was followed by a long series on cells, starting with a quote from R. D. Laing: 'I, as I write this…am a collection of cells (in the order of 2^{64+}…) all of which count one cell, forty eight years ago as our common ancestor.'[14] It quickly became obvious that this many cells would actualy fill a cube around one hundred feet in diameter. Thus I revised the estimate downwards to 6×10^{12} cells, welcoming the presence of error and uncertainty from the start. As mentioned above, I went on to consider astronomical and geophysical questions. Here is an example of the kind of poem that resulted from these activities:

WORLD WAR II

Fifty-five million people were killed
at a cost per corpse of over
a quarter of a million dollars,
a third their weight in gold.

Which took a total firepower of three megatons.
Which is the energy
of a seven minute hurricane
or of one hour of the world's tides.

Who got a mention?
The history book names 117
or one in half a million.

The advantages
a rise in technology
massive development in agriculture.

Indeed, by the equivalence of matter and energy
the firepower condenses to the mass
of a small potato.

How much does this represent
of all the energy used in human history?

Compare an electric fire to an earthquake
or a full stop to a small dog.

The graveyard would cover an entire city.
The gold would fill

In the course of this I needed to find the price of gold in 1945. It seems that its value was set by the President of the U.S., who arrived at the figure by asking his wife to guess a number before they went to sleep at night.

Perhaps she dreams Freud loses all his money / in a telepathy scam[15]. After working on purely physical features for so long, I became interested in the size of the mind. Estimates of the flux of information through the senses are huge. Whether one considers the number of rods and cones in the retina and their powers of resolution, or the cellular economy of the eye, which is sensitive enough to detect a single photon in complete darkness, or the number of sensory neural connections and the rate at which they fire, the amount of information entering the eye appears to be of the order of one gigabyte per second. (Including the other senses using similar methods does not increase this estimate appreciably.) I find this very exciting, especially in a society where we are more concerned to evaluate than to value people. What a piece of work is anyone.

The point of music is constantly vanishing[16]. The obvious question was, where does it all go? How much do we remember, at any level? I read quite a number of books on memory in pursuit of this question. Unfortunately, most of them seemed more concerned with forgetting.

I was intrigued by Wilder Penfield's findings. The brain, being devoid of pain sensors, can be operated on directly, without any anaesthetic. *While operating on epileptic patients, Penfield applied electric currents to the brain's surface in order to find problem areas. Since the patients were awake during the operations, they could tell Penfield what they were experiencing. Probing some areas would trigger whole memory sequences. For one patient, Penfield triggered a familiar song that sounded so clear, the patient thought it was being played in the operating room.*[17] In other words, patients didn't just 'remember' experiences but re-lived them, re-experiencing all the sights, sounds, smells and other sensations as well as thoughts and emotions. I remember reading too of a woman admitted to Casualty, apparently delirious, speaking in an unknown language. By chance someone recognised that she was speaking Homeric Greek. It turned out she worked as a cleaner, one of her clients being a classics student who used to recite the *Iliad* and the *Odyssey* in preparation for tests. Finally, the state-of-the-art levels of virtual reality that the average person routinely achieves in dreams, far outstripping anything silicon has done, suggests a higher capacity for memory than one might ordinarily imagine.

The brain, representing only 2% of the body's mass, uses 20% of our glucose intake. Only 10% of this is required for cellular subsistence. Suppose the rest is devoted to cognitive activity. Taking the energy required to process 1 bit of information as 10^{-19} joules (roughly the energy of a visible photon, or the energy transferred by one molecule of ATP, or the minimum energy required to cross a synapse), this would lead to a mental activity level of 10^{20} bits per second. Various different starting assumptions lead to a similar value. This is considerably bigger than the sensory flux. It is as if each second the brain generates the equivalent of decades of experience.

Steven Rose estimates the actual activity of the conscious mind as 100 bits per second. The comparison of this to the figures for sensory flux and mental processing is even more striking, something along the lines of thimble, cathedral and ocean. Which brings me back to the question raised earlier: how is communication possible? Given the amount of processing which so vastly outstrips the senses, what is there to stop us disappearing into our own private ocean? Indeed, what is there to stop us abandoning any semblance of reality for a private fantasy? Clearly this is an option. But what prevents it from being obligatory?

One answer is to consider that the mind is itself a natural phenomenon. Our division between the artificial and the natural, while having profound (or profoundly shallow) political implications, may be something of a fantasy itself. Perhaps a poem, sexual preference or dinner menu can be no more artificial than a spider web. Thus our worlds, each a work of art, must at least begin in the real. This is unsatisfactory in many ways, and does little to answer the sceptical philosophers.

Another, less trivial, answer is to consider the human population. There was a time, not so long ago, when humanity had the status of an endangered species. (I'm not suggesting that this is no longer true.) The world population would have been numbered in the thousands. Since the family tree of any individual expands as you go back in time, yet the overall population contracts, this means that branches must be shared. We are far more related than we think. It has been calculated that an arbitrarily chosen couple must be at least 50th cousins. I would entertain hopes of bringing that limit in closer. In any case, this would suggest that, for all their explosive power, the way minds construct their versions of reality must have common ground.

> terrible fashions
> consciousness
> fashions consciousness[18]

Given the grandeur of the human mind, 10^{20} b.p.s. in the model above, one might ask why consciousness is so relatively puny. Why a bubble floating in all that cognitive space? Perhaps we need to reduce our interior awareness, to avoid complete paralysis in the face of the simplest decisions. A highly filtered subset of the sense flux is prioritised, disproportionately in terms of magnitude, but not in terms of survival. In positive terms it is a lifeline, ensuring we have some connection with 'reality'. Obviously, it is important not to be lost in one's own innards if there are tigers on the prowl. But as with pain, sometimes nature overdoes things. Our insensitivity to our own vastness causes us to persistently underestimate people, especially other people.

I say these things not because they happen / but because many things happen.[19] One of the things I like about the calculations above is the way they treat error. The assumptions behind them are an interesting mix of the precise and the speculative. For instance, one of the variables in standard calculations of the probability of the existence of intelligent life on other planets is particularly fuzzy. This can lead to the conclusion that the Earth is an isolated example, as if life were so improbable that an entire universe is required in order to have one sentient planet, or that we inhabit a packed cosmos in which one can hardly get a word in edgeways. Nevertheless, even at their most speculative, these false facts, number pictures aim for clarity, even if that means being clearly wrong.[20] And this clarity is a rich source of further questions. Small errors in the transcription of genes fuel evolution. Without error the process would grind to a halt.[21] Without uncertainty, matter would collapse.[22] It's a small step to consider randomness as the engine of the world. However, diversity is expensive. Nature is far from green, is indifferent to waste and, like doctors, buries its mistakes. One reason living beings appear to be so perfect, so exquisitely designed, is that the construction lines have been erased. *In a completely blind process anything, even vision, is possible.*[23] Yes, but at the cost of deaths on a massive scale. Evolution is not progress.[24] Without the 'mistakes' that died along the way, there would be no 'successes'. In any case, such parenthetical terms are worse than meaningless, and only the present mania for continually comparing the incommensurable gives them any plausibility. Every living thing is priceless, incomparably.

Million-fuelèd, | *nature's bonfire burns on.*[25] That order can arise from random processes is intriguing. Many definitions of randomness focus on the product. For example, a sequence is called random if it cannot be represented by any description shorter than the sequence itself. By this light the sequence H, T, H, T, H, T, H, T, etc. is not random. I am not entirely happy with a definition that excludes origins in this way. Clearly this *could* be the outcome of repeatedly tossing a coin. *Nymph on a sampan nirvana audits til tigress*[26]. Opposites have the interesting habit of turning into each other. Can we know whether a given pattern is the result of chance, is a distortion imposed by our perception, or reflects something in nature? This has consequences for how we read. How may we gauge a writer's intentions? Is the poem bounded by these in any case?[27] How far can we go?[28]

 A common-sense | *Thumbs down on the dodo's mode.*[29] When we discovered that our second daughter, Florence, was deaf, we contacted the deaf community and arranged to be taught sign language at home. Our teacher, Wendy Murray, was superb. Gradually, we realised that sign language is prohibited in Ireland.[30] One shocking detail after another emerged. I remember signing with a deaf man, a big strong intelligent chap, plasterer by trade, and he was reduced to tears by the memory of having his hands tied behind his back in school to stop him signing. He is a deaf son of deaf parents and just couldn't keep his hands quiet, no matter how often warned to "use his voice". In recent years he has been involved in the independent Irish Deaf Society which, unlike the older National Association of the Deaf, is run by the deaf. When Florence was about six I began to write a poem, *Arbor Vitae*[31], based on our experience. I wanted every detail to be as vibrant and alive as possible, reflecting the tremendous vivacity of our deaf friends. This meant that any technique used had to earn its keep. The anagrams of the word 'chaos' in section one have a number of different purposes. Fundamentally, anagrams recall life's movement across generations, as 'letters' in various genes shift position. Here, they also represented the way an overdose of order descends into chaos. Instructions are given for working out the 120 anagrams, mirroring the way those in institutions are constantly given instruction. They are also a metaphor for branching, twigs on the word branch. Then again, they act as a musical device, the birds in the tree as Maurice Scully once wrote in a letter. In each section there are several acrostics, each a gesture of solidarity in that they will be silent in any reading, no matter how good your hearing is. They also allow the inclusion of horizontal / vertical, mirroring the Irish sign for YES, and commenting on the religious background via the traditional idea of the Christian cross as a sign of contradiction in which these opposing directions meets. There is also the idea of history as the vertical and the present as the horizontal, etc.

Jangling the metal of the strings...[32] I am interested in establishing as many dialogues between form and theme as possible. As with natural form (natural in the traditional as well as the expanded sense above), this may imply a simple plan, the details of which continually open onto other details. Not so much an onion as a bush, with a readily apprehensible outline, its finer divisions going in every direction. I don't expect the reader to sit with a magnifying glass and geometrical instruments plotting every tangent. But they're there. And they happen naturally enough. Writing is not entirely conscious. Very few activities of any interest are. A technique like this is an act of faith in the magnificence of the human brain, anyone's brain. Perception is a creative act, far outpacing the capabilities of camera, mike and other sensors. How can one not be poetic with minds so nimble and vast? Anyone who wants to can realise a valid reading of any text,[33] unless they have been convinced otherwise, or unless they have a specific difficulty with texts in general. No matter how many relationships a text may hold, it's peanuts compared with the intricacies we negotiate as we go to answer the front door. And as with writing, reading does not have to be entirely conscious. That said, while Florence's hearing has improved as she's gotten older, suggesting her deafness was obstructive rather than neural, she is also mentally handicapped,[34] and has taught us that there's a lot more to life than reading.

I would consider technique to be an unreliable fence if you wish to carve up the landscape of poetry. The alternation of prose and verse is beautifully handled in Boethius' *The Consolation of Philosophy*. Dense argument flows passionately through Lucretius' *On the Nature of the Universe*. Random methods, whether in divination poems or as part of biology, have an ancient history. Collage was almost *de rigeur* among Renaissance Latinists. The erasure of self was as near complete as it can be among the *Fiannaíochta*[35] poems of the early middle ages. (Though given the nature of mind, I can hardly conceive of any human gesture that does not contain some element of autobiography.) The surreal has to work hard to beat nursery rhymes, never mind the awesome oddness of the simply literal.

random intelligence echoes planets and stars[36]. It's late now. When Louise and I were first married we used to read to each other at night, one of the books being Spenser's *The Faerie Queene*. In one episode the Redcrosse Knight is stuck in a wandering wood, which allegedly represents error. *in the tree's underchamber / the roots enmesh and thicken*[37]. Interestingly, woods *can* wander. Even over decades. Many of the world's processes occur on time-scales which are not easily measured by a human pulse. Constellations, genes, languages all drift beyond the range of our ideas of permanence. At the other extreme are processes so rapid, evanescent, yet fundamental, that we hardly guess their existence. Incomplete, uncertain, tenacious, dense and diverse. With a beat. Beatrice is asleep in an armchair, her eyelids fluttering. I'd like to close with a piece that occurred to me in a dream.[38]

Mutability Checkers

The full deck gusts outside the playground
briefly forming an aerial house of cards.
I see a woodlouse chasing a tiger,
and square pegs in square holes.
An atom is the part of your throat that sticks out.
Every Saturday, I am a bicycle.
Famous Dialogues lie on a table.
Enter Socrates, winged by the medium's
dot to dot. Solvent without solution,
ignoramus champ of all history,
I think of you sending away a would-be
empiricist with a flea in his ear,
then sweeping to the end of the argument –
reality as a series of diagrams.
Secateured titan, I dreamed a random river
whose surface's inflexions shimmered
with every possible geometry
where all-envisaging blindness hatched
and crossed as chance, swollen with potential,
surged against the given, sculpting a world
where botched and sublime bloomed without design

Notes

[1]William Carlos Williams. *Smell!*

[2]William Blake. *The Marriage of Heaven and Hell*. London and New York: Longman, 1989, Section III, Proverbs of Hell, line 8.

[3]Randolph Healy. 'This Size of This Universe', *Other: British and Irish Poetry Since 1970*, Richard Caddel and Peter Quartermain, editors. New England: Wesleyan University Press, 1999, 114.

[4]Bertrand Russell. *History of Western Philosophy*. London: Unwin Paperbacks, 1980, 13.

[5]Eavan Boland. 'The Woman Changes her Skin', *Collected Poems*. Manchester: Carcanet, 1995, 86.

[6]Seamus Heaney. 'The Railway Children', *New Selected Poems 1996-1987*. London: Faber and Faber, 1988, 159.

[7]Dermot Bolger. '1966', *Taking My Letters Back*. Dublin: New Island Books, 1998, 51.

[8]Trevor Joyce. ' '93/94', *stone floods*. Dublin and Cork: New Writers Press, 1995, 37

[9]Peter Riley. *Untitled Sequence*. Bray, Co. Wicklow, Ireland: Wild Honey Press, 1999, 5.

[10]Steve McCaffery. *Evoba*. Toronto: The Coach House Press, 1987, 14.

[11]Suppose $p^2 = 2$ and $p = a/b$, where nothing greater than 1 divides both a and b evenly, i.e. the ratio has been 'broken down'. Thus $p^2 = a^2/b^2 = 2$, that is, $a^2 = 2b^2$, which means that a^2 is even. Thus a is even (since the square of an odd number is odd), hence there must be a whole number k so that $a = 2k$. Squaring we get $a^2 = 4k^2$. From the penultimate equation we have $4k^2 = 2b^2$, which can be simplified to yield $2k^2 = b^2$. Thus b^2 and hence b is even. This means that both a and b can be divided evenly by 2, which contradicts the statement that the highest number that does so is 1. Thus the square root of 2 is irrational. This proof was known to the Greeks.

[12]The most famous of these concerns the set of all sets which do not contain themselves. Russell gives the example of the set of all teaspoons. This does not contain itself, since it is not a teaspoon. Put all such sets together into one enormous collection: the set of all sets which do not contain themselves. Does this giant contain itself? If it doesn't, well it should, since its job is to contain all those sets which don't. But if it does then it shouldn't because then it wouldn't be a set that didn't contain itself. They're still at the drawing board on this one.

[13]Tom Raworth. 'Emptily', *Clean & Well Lit*. New York: Roof Books, 1996, 63.

[14]R. D. Laing. *The Facts of Life*. Harmondwsorth: Penguin, 1976, 26. This is a beautiful book and I'd not wish to give the impression that the only thing I got out of it was a mistake.

[15]Penelope Shuttle. 'Tigers', *Selected Poems 1980 – 1996*. Oxford and New York: Oxford Poets, 1998, 94.

[16]Rosmarie Waldrop. 'Conversation 20: On Pattern', *Reluctant Gravities*. New York, New Directions, 1999, 79.

[17]See the website *http://www.pbs.org/wgbh/aso/tryit/brain/cortexhistory2.html* for more information.

[18]Catherine Walsh. I*dir Eatortha and Making Tents*. London: Invisible Books, 1996, 32.

[19]Lee Ann Brown. *Crush*. New York: Leave Books, 1993, 13.

[20]From time to time I check my own calculations. On one of these forays I discovered that a metaphor used in World War II above is incorrect. So I left it that way.

[21]Apparently able to decline the offer of evolving, snails will only mate with other snails above a certain temperature. The entire population of snails north of a line through Scotland is thus composed of billions of clones.

[22]Negatively charged electrons can be thought of as orbiting a positively charged nucleus. So why don't they just stick together? The diameter of a nucleus is of the order

of 10^{-15} m. According to Heisenberg's principle the uncertainties in the electron's position and momentum must have a minimum product. In order to be located in so precise an area as a nucleus, an electron would thus have to have a speed in excess of that of light *in vacuo*. Which would violate the theory of relativity. Uncertainty stops atoms from collapsing.

[23]Jacques Monod. *Chance and Necessity*.

[24]Those who regard humanity as the peak of a hierarchy might consider that the process continues and the 'peak' will eventually be superseded.

[25]Gerard Manley Hopkins. 'THAT NATURE IS A HERACLITEAN FIRE AND OF THE COMFORT OF THE RESURRECTION', *Poems and Prose*, selected by W. H. Gardner. Harmondsworth: Penguin Books, 1979, 66.

[26]Karen Mac Cormack. 'Export Notwithstanding', *Marine Snow*. Toronto: ECW Press, 1995, 49.

[27]One might note that in current practice if a sublime construction may be put on a text the credit is as likely to go to the critic as the writer. However, any bigotry imputed is placed firmly on the writer's doorstep. All things being equal, this would give the author a responsibility quotient of 75 %.

[28]I remember in class once a German student, pen poised, asked "What is the correct interpretation of this poem?" Hard not to be struck at how neatly this summarises a wide range of issues.

[29]Sylvia Plath. 'You're', *Ariel*. London: Faber and Faber, 1968, 57.

[30]Much of the history behind this prohibition is documented in Sarah E. Burns' 'Irish Sign Language in a Minority Language Framework', submitted to Trinity College Dublin as her M.Sc. Thesis in April 1995.

[31]The full text is available at **http://www.wildhoneypress.com**

[32]Wallace Stevens. 'The Man with the Blue Guitar', *Selected Poems*. London: Faber and Faber, 1956, 52.

[33]All the same, I have often been surprised at how many people persist in reading poetry as if it had no rhythm.

[34]The Irish association for people like Flo went through an enormous amount of heart searching to find the current term: learning disabled. Neither she, nor her peers, were in a position to comment. It struck me at the time that such concerns, while motivated by care, can go too far. There's nothing wrong with Flo being the way she is. No euphemism required.

[35]These recount the exploits of Fionn Mac Cumhail (Finn McCoole) and his fellow warriors. Their form is rigorously legislated.

[36]Joan Retallack. *Afterrimages*. Hanover and London: Wesleyan University Press, 1995, 9.

[37]Maurice Scully. 'RESPONSIBILITY', *STEPS*. London: Reality Street Editions, 1998, 30.

[38]Randolph Healy. *Rana Rana!*. Bray, Co. Wicklow, Ireland: Wild Honey Press, 1997, 5.

Michael S. Begnal

Idir Dhá Thine Bhealtaine

Gearóid Mac Lochlainn, *Sruth Teangacha / Stream of Tongues*, Cló Iar-
Chonnachta, pb., €15.

The publication of this bilingual volume of selected poems from
Belfast Irish-language poet Gearóid Mac Lochlainn is as welcome as it
is problematic. A voice which has heretofore been missing from
contemporary Irish literary discourse, that of the Northern Gaeilgeoir,
can finally claim its rightful place on the main stage. In a world
dominated by now middle-aged poets like Ní Dhomhnaill, Ó
Searcaigh and Davitt, Mac Lochlainn's voice is the voice of youth. His
confidence echoes that of his people in the North who know that their
day will come. You could say that Mac Lochlainn's has arrived.

Sruth Teangacha / Stream of Tongues is a book that works on several
different levels. The original poems are composed in an assured free
verse where the poet allows the euphony of the Irish language to
unfurl of its own accord. He moves easily from childhood reminis-
cence to pub sessions, from the Troubles to meditations on the artistic
process itself. Mac Lochlainn is an urban writer with a healthy
disregard for the sometimes choking weight of Gaelic tradition:

> ...life's too short to get hung up
> on Old Irish, Middle Irish,
> syllable and metre
> and that long-in-the-tooth old hag –
> the traditional thing.
> I can't stand here lowing the
> Och Och ón either...
> — 'Poet's Choice'

The Irish that has taken root in West Belfast has necessarily
developed along its own path, its own dirty concrete streets. It is
informed by Gaeltacht Irish but no longer in thrall to it. Thus Mac
Lochlainn writes, 'I once had a girl, / a fine, fit-looking girl. / She was a
native speaker / but her kisses tasted / as sweet / as any other.' ('The
Native Speaker'). Mac Lochlainn's awareness that his Irish is not 'native',
in the Gaeltacht sense, fosters the edgy, energetic quality in his writing.

But it is the tension between the Irish and English languages that is really at the heart of Mac Lochlainn's poetry. As a native of Belfast – a part of the country still occupied by British military forces – Mac Lochlainn cannot help but be confronted by questions of cultural and linguistic identity. The poem 'Rite of Passage' describes the first time its speaker is stopped by a British army patrol: '– Keep yer fucking 'ands on the wall, Paddy! // I heard my details passed over the radio / to another stranger at base, / my Irish name now unrecognisable, / carved up by the crackling blades of English and static.' The ongoing British occupation of the North is here analogous to the often antagonistic relationship between the two languages, the indigenous Irish and the colonizing English. It is a duality that of course extends to the whole country, arguably present in the psyche of every Irish person since Hugh O'Neill. Mac Lochlainn embodies it and makes it a source of poetry.

The question of translation has always been a dilemma for the writer of Irish. English translations have the advantageous effect of making an Irish-language poet accessible to the wider world, as Nuala Ní Dhomhnaill is quick to point out in her foreword to this book. (As great a poet as she is, she obviously would not be where she is today if not for translation.) Mac Lochlainn does not shy away from the inherent difficulties of translation, or pretend that the English versions can ever be the equivalent of the Irish. As he writes in his own Author's Notes, 'In the original poems sound shaped syntax to a large extent and for this reason I believe it is impossible to really 'translate' Irish poetry… While translation may get close to what is signified by the original words there is always a loss of music.' Languages are not merely collections of words with direct correlation to each other, as anyone who speaks more than one language knows. Instead each one encapsulates a specific world-view inherent in its grammar and idiom; each defines a unique mode of consciousness.

Mac Lochlainn therefore views the translations as 'cover versions' of the originals, to continue the musical analogy. The English versions, often translated or co-translated by the poet himself, along with Frank Sewell, Ciaran Carson, Medbh McGuckian, Rita Kelly, Gabriel Rosenstock, Pearse Hutchinson and others, form an extension of the original Irish poems but do not cling to them. In some places they differ significantly. To return to 'Rite of Passage', the original poems ends,

> Ní dhearna mé dearmad ar an lá sin
> ag dul chun na scoile,

ceithre bliana déag d'aois,
mé ag teacht in oirbheart,

an chéad uair a mhothaigh mé
snáthaid ghéar náire, faobhar fuar fuatha,
céadtuiscint
ar an fhocal –
Éireannach.

A literal translation of these lines might be rendered, 'I haven't forgotten that day / going to school, / 14 years old, / on the brink of manhood, / / the first time I felt / the sharp needle of shame, the cold edge of hate, / first understanding / of the word / "Irish." ' However, Mac Lochlainn's own translation of the same section is given as follows:

That was that, as they say,
pimpled pubescent, teeny-bob,
slugging a trail to school,
scalpeled tongue,
the hypodermics
of military operations,
a first stab
at translation.

There are any number of possible reasons for such a radical departure, not least of which is contained in the Author's Notes where Mac Lochlainn writes of 'a playful jibe thrown out at the monoglot who seeks truth in translation.'

In another instance, the original is actually 'improved' by the translation. 'Ag Siopadóireacht / Shopping' describes a scene, witnessed by the speaker and his friend, of a nationalist youth running and escaping from an RUC-man. 'Yesss! a ghlaoigh Mo Chara, a dhorn san aer, "Tiocfaidh ár lá!" / Is d'imigh muid linn thar Halla na Cathrach / lena Union Jack cromtha...', it reads in the Irish. The English version, however, reads, 'Yesss! yelled Mo Chara, fisting the air, "Tiocfaidh ár lá!" / And off we went past the City Hall / where the Union Jack hung limp and forlorn...' The Irish word cromtha means simply 'bent', or 'stooped'. But the Union Jack '[hanging] limp and forlorn', the one word expanded to three, gives a much more definite impression of waning British dominance in the North. Especially when contrasted with the power of the exclamation Tiocfaidh ár lá!, and the fist in the air (the fist of revolution), it makes for an incredibly vivid image. It is present in the Irish of course, but there it is somewhat more subtle.

For the bilingual reader of *Sruth Teangacha / Stream of Tongues*, the Irish and English versions play off each other in just this manner. Read this way, the book becomes a sort of meta-work, composed not of Irish poems and English translations, but of the interaction between the two (and the spoken renditions on the accompanying CD add yet another dimension). But the thing is that neither the originals nor the translations can any longer be considered authoritative in their own right. While each version adds something to its counterpart, it also undermines any claim that either might have to being the 'real' poem. Certainly this is the effect Mac Lochlainn intended in regard to the translations – he speaks here of the danger of allowing the English versions to 'gain an autonomy of their own and eclipse the Irish' (something which seems to have happened to Ní Dhomhnaill, for example). What may be unintended is the effect on the original works. For the Irish-speaker, who of course speaks English too, the knowledge that a 'parallel' version exists destabilizes the authority of the original just as much as vice versa. There can be no wilful ignorance: no sooner have you read even the title of a poem than your eyes glance over to see how it was translated. This is a predicament which did not apply to Mac Lochlainn's first two all-Irish collections (*Babylon Gaeilgeoir* and *Na Scéalaithe*), from which the present volume derives. But in the case of *Sruth Teangacha / Stream of Tongues*, there is no going back.

What saves this collection from collapsing under the weight of its own contradictions is the fact that, simply put, this is reality for many people. A bit like watching TG4, with its ubiquitous English subtitles. Mac Lochlainn's book reflects a process of perception in the subtitled Gaelic mind that has been developing for decades now, for centuries even, dictated by the minority position of the Irish language in an English-speaking world. At the same time, such a work is an inherent challenge to the false sense of security enjoyed by the monolingual English-speaker. 'Sometimes, you get tired of talking / to lazy Irish ears. Tired / of self-satisfied monoglots who say / – *It sounds lovely. I wish I had the Irish. / Don't you do translations?*' writes Mac Lochlainn in the ironical 'Translations'. He does do translations as it turns out, but they are often of the type that subverts just such a question. *Sruth Teangacha / Stream of Tongues* thus stands as a significant evolutionary marker not only in Irish-language literature, but in Irish literature as a whole.

Eamon Grennan

The Double Existence

Seamus Heaney, *Finders Keepers: Selected Prose 1971—2001*, Faber & Faber, hb., stg€20.
Dennis O'Driscoll, *Troubled Thoughts, Majestic Dreams: Selected Prose Writings*, Gallery Books, pb., €17.50

When Keats said that 'Shakespeare lived a life of allegory; his works are the comments on it', he provided a brilliant formulation for the understanding of the relationship between the life and work of any artist. The truth is, of course, that everyone leads a life of allegory. To be human is to live the facts and seek the meanings: allegory amounts to a specific version of this double existence. But only writers leave behind them the 'comment on it' that is composed of their work. I was particularly reminded of this remark of Keats when I came across, on the first page of *Finders Keepers*, Seamus Heaney's account of an early memory (that could be 'half-dream', or he 'may even be imagining it'). It is a moment that lends itself very easily to the notion of a life as allegory: The poet remembers 'a green web, a caul of veined light, a tangle of rods and pods, stalks and tendrils, full of assuaging earth and leaf smell, a sunlit lair. I'm sitting as if just awakened from a winter sleep and gradually become aware of voices, coming closer, calling my name, and for no reason at all I have begun to weep.' Like the action of Yeats's 'The Stolen Child', and as surely as any of the epiphanies in Wordsworth's *Prelude*, this moment – with its 'caul' and its 'lair' (and in a nearby sentence the phrase 'secret nests') – is a moment of symbolic birth: the birth of both the self-delighting imagination immersed in its own green world, and then the summoning of that imagination into the realm of ordinary life. Those voices calling his name; that weeping for no apparent cause: what Heaney registers here is the instant of *vocation* (a word with its root in voice, in calling, and branching off into, among other things, religion). And in this case it is a vocation that compels in him an awareness of the double life of the imagination, the necessary coexistence in it of rapture and responsibility, the peculiar, human cost of it all.

Much of Heaney's being as a poet could be summarized in this emblematic moment, in the way it pictures an absorption in the self's own enchanted freedom being resisted by the force of another, external need. Think of the poem 'Exposure' in *North*, which locates the poet among 'alders dripping, birches / Inheriting the last light', where he is 'weighing and weighing / My responsible *tristia*. / For what? For the ear? For the people?' And what is *Station Island* if not a penitential sequence of such 'callings', a sequence that ends with the figure of James Joyce – archbishop of heretical vocations – ordaining the shriven, 'convalescent' poet into a new and riskier independence of imaginative commitment? And since this present selection of his essays and lecture shows, as Heaney himself says, 'how one poet answered poetry's call', these prose pieces might be seen as part of that vocational waking to the world, part of the way this poet exercises (and, maybe, exorcises) his sense of the responsibility of the calling.

Culled from his three earlier collections (*Preoccupations, The Government of the Tongue,* and *The Redress of Poetry*), as well as including some previously uncollected pieces, this *Selected Prose* presents in sharp outline the fact that what all Heaney's discursive writing adds up to is a steady, coherent, late twentieth-century 'Apology for Poetry' or 'Defense of Poetry'. Like Sidney and like Shelley, Heaney is preoccupied with the place of poetry in the world. In his introduction to this volume he quotes his own words from the Foreword to *Preoccupations*: 'How should a poet properly live and write? What is his relationship to be to his own voice, his own place, his literary heritage and his contemporary world.' Such words underline the essentially moral nature of the poetic project, or insist on the necessary coexistence in it of ethical and aesthetic considerations. Binocular in vision, stereophonic in audition, these essays of close attention keep reminding us that poetry is an art whose end is pleasure but whose consequence must, if it is to be of true human value, broaden beyond the satisfactions of the ear and the nervous system towards addressing something in the moral nature, towards making the sort of sense we'd call (and probably mean a number of things by calling) spiritual. As Heaney's own poems might be said to embody interrogative, often anxious reflections on their own being, on their 'authority' in the nightmare world of history, these essays also act out in prose ponderings and investigations some implicit answers to Adorno's question regarding the possibility of poetry after the Holocaust. What the essays show – whether their subject is Kavanagh or Mandelstam, Bishop or Muldoon, Yeats or Mahon or Longley, Kinsella or Dante, George or

Zbigniew Herbert, John Clare or Burns or Plath or Milosz – is what the *art* in poetry is, and how it is *as art* that poetry contains and exercises its moral efficacy. I suppose this could be called 'sacramental criticism': the good poem's body of language – in its sonic pitch and its rhythmic pull – becoming 'the outward sign of an inward grace', a grace that amplifies inside us as we read, and opens us by its own kinds of confirmation and surprise to a larger, deeper and more aware participation in the world.

Of course as soon as I see that term 'sacramental criticism' I can hear the author of the essays saying, 'Come off it!' For one of the most engaging aspects of these pages is the way they demonstrate Heaney's own impatience with bullshit, his antennae always turned back on himself, insisting that whatever rapt intellectual flights he might engage in, he must stay grounded in a common idiom of appreciation, tuned to and often operating in the currency of the works which he's discussing. The essays, so, have the sound of a person talking his thoughts into the world and into our minds, proceeding at a deftly measured pace, never losing his readers in the mists of jargon or numbing them with intellectual ether for its own sake. Again and again he reminds us of the physical properties of poetry, of how it is located first in the body, in the larynx, in the beating heart. So the essays are a pleasure to go back to, their eloquence always exercised on behalf of some useful revelation. They show a constancy of genial enthusiasm given heft and ballast by the purposeful, patently serious but never over-earnest bent of an intelligence and a sensibility working together. I love their *vocabulary*, how plain words like 'ply' or 'stir,' 'lift-off', 'nimble' or 'roughage' are allied to the higher register of phrases like 'discreet immensity', 'phonetic jewel' or unpuzzling mysteriousness'. Through this and through the muscular vivacity and syntactic visibility of Heaney's sentences, the prose pieces become the satisfying shadow to the body of poems created by *Opened Ground: Selected poems 1966-1996*. The thirty years of poems are matched by the thirty years of prose, so that between them they compose a full-length portrait of a distinct, generous, tirelessly engaged imagination at work in the world.

Since this is a *Selection*, I should quickly get out of the way my regrets about exclusions. I miss especially the essay on Hopkins from *Preoccupations*, since Heaney drew a deal of inspirational (and possibly cautionary) light from his tough-minded meditation on the verbal volatility and intensely Catholic apprehensions of the author of 'The Windhover', 'Felix Randall', 'The Wreck of the Deutschland', and the 'terrible' sonnets. I also miss the essay on Osip and Nadezhda Mandelstam, since the work of the Russian poet is – along with Yeats and Milosz, Dante's *Commedia*, the poems and letters of Keats, Wordsworth's *Prelude*, and Rilke's *Sonnets to Orpheus* – among Heaney's sacred texts. But in any selection sacrifices have to be made. What's important is the way the selection itself is a willed configuration of meanings, a self-profile of sorts, which we can look at, wonder about.

Heaney's criticism is a refined, robust mixture of subjectivity and objectivity, determined to celebrate or at least appreciate whatever imaginative projects he brings under scrutiny. Of course any poet's criticism is likely to be in some way, however oblique, a kind of justification of his or her own work. (The criticism, that is, can help us read and understand the poems.) But while this must be so in Heaney's case, his criticism is always performed with both eyes wide open on, and his imaginative conscience responsive to, the figure of justice standing behind 'justification', ever alert to the Yeatsian injunction about holding reality and justice in a single thought. In fact it's his generosity as a critic that impresses me most, I think, the way he allows us, by sharing his rich insights (as poet and reader, as teacher) to participate in the life of what he is talking about. He becomes, as a reader-critic, a pathway to the heart of his subject. He does not stand in its way or in our way, casting over it some thick, solipsistic shadow of himself. Whether leaning into the work of Kavanagh or Larkin, Bishop or Lowell or Hughes, his explorations always seem to touch something at the heart of the poet he's reading, but without any irritable attempt to pluck out the heart of his or her mystery. Rather he will *essay* to understand what he might seem least sympathetic to (as he does, for example, in his reading of 'Aubade', Philip Larkin's 'definitive post-Christian English poem'), taking on forces which most oppose his own way into the world, using the criticism to say what his own poems might appear to be denying or ignoring.

These, too, are the essays and lectures of a teacher. Not an 'academic' – since that word has been so devalued in the literary marketplace – but a teacher, one who brings the word 'professor' back to its roots in the verb. In an essay called 'On Poetry and Professing', he observes that the advantage a poet teaching literature or poetry can have 'is the fact that he or she is likely to possess a credible personal language . . .there will be no gap between the professional idiom and the personal recognitions.' It is precisely here that his own criticism seems to me so distinguished. He manages to marry professional idiom to personal recognitions so no gap appears between them. He has had the courage of his convictions, and has found and wrought a language to – aptly and adequately – embody them. In a discussion of Christopher Marlowe, for example, he confronts some of the posturings of literary political correctness. Despite the bloodied colonial reputation of poets like Marlowe, Raleigh or Spenser – which he acknowledges – he can stand his ground as poet-appreciator by saying 'it still seems an abdication of literary responsibility to be swayed by these desperately overdue correctives [of post-colonial readings] to a point where imaginative literature is read simply and solely as a function of an oppressive discourse, or as a reprehensible masking.' His is a critical attitude that wants to get 'past the glissando of post-modernism and get stuck in the mud of real imaginative haulage.' In his work as critic, teacher, and (I want to say) *philosopher* of poetry, he proves just how richly professional idiom and personal recognitions have cross-pollinated to produce one of the most nourishing, lasting, and genuinely illuminating bodies of contemporary critical literature. So it's appropriate that he ends the collection with praise of Milosz, for it is this tersely epigrammatic observation of Milosz's that is one of Heaney's touchstones of value in what he does: 'But poetry by its very essence', says Milosz, 'is on the side of life.' It is an interesting step from Arnold's sense of poetry as 'a criticism of life', to Milosz's poetry 'on the side of life.' Maybe a step from the Nineteenth to the Twentieth century. Whatever about that, for Milosz, for Heaney, this is what poetry and its 'professors' teach.

One of the more noticeable aspects of this selection is the way it underlines Heaney's determination to create his own space, and how precisely that space is aligned. He has been, in the words of Dennis O'Driscoll, 'an exemplary practitioner of poetry in a time of conflict', trying, as he says himself, to keep a humane perspective and 'at the same time grant the religious intensity of the violence its authenticity and complexity.' The essays, implicitly, are a way of Heaney holding his own ground. Putting his autobiographical pieces on growing up in

County Derry and then in Belfast alongside his public quarrel with being called a 'British' poet; remarking, in an essay on Larkin and Hill and Hughes, the way English poets investigate not only the matter of England but 'what is the matter with England' (the unspoken fact being Northern Ireland); probing the language of Burns and John Clare – in all such projects he carefully positions himself inside his unquestionable sense of being Irish, while at the same time staking a claim to the English tradition (an act of reverse appropriation consummated, I guess, in his translation of *Beowulf*). There is never any doubt about which 'side' of the vicious divides in the North he *comes from*, no matter how hard through his exemplary work as poet, critic, inescapably public figure he has laboured towards the healing of those divisions. A recurrent stress in the essays is the fact that it is in language itself that Heaney often sees the Northern situation, in its roots and in its potential remedies. Not that it is just a matter of words, but that a right use of the inherited language or languages could open minds and hearts to the necessarily mixed nature of culture and people in the North, and that this sense of mixture would be a possible path towards tolerance, towards the kinds of mutual acknowledgement of what he calls 'throughotherness' – that 'interinanimation' (John Donne's word) needed if there is to be any cure. At the same time, however, this selection of his work underlines the fact that it is not only as a Northerner that he wishes to be understood. Always resistant to the idea of poetry 'as a quest for political attitudes', his career is itself a ramifying from those personal, familial, tribal roots towards the broader identity he feels as that 'veritable human being' he refers to in concluding his Nobel address, 'Crediting Poetry'.

It was Keats who spoke of the 'fine excess' that poetry needed, and there is something of such 'fine excess' about many of these prose pieces. Whether talking about Mahon's 'displaced consciousness' or Muldoon's 'violent and resourceful fantasy' or the 'tender insinuation and possibility' in the cadences of Michael Longley, it is Heaney's special gift to discover simple but polished formulations that seem exactly right. What seems most important to me is that these essays and lectures (the lecture format permitting him a kind of creative relaxation in the face of difficult matter) always make me want to find the book or play or poem in question, and to read or re-read it by the light of his genially penetrating response to its possibilities. But, beyond that pleasure, what he manages to show in all of these pieces, in their aesthetic judgements as well as in their ability to move from the inner ring of aesthetics to outer rings of politics and morality, is how poetry, in the words of Geoffrey Hill, 'is responsible. It is a form of responsible behaviour, not a directive.' Had Yeats not claimed it first, it seems to me this selected prose could have moved quite comfortably under the title, *Responsibilities* (though I suspect, with his inclining towards mischief, that Heaney might have added *and Irresponsibilities*). No matter. What does matter is that with that 'labour and perseverance' which he praises in Yeats, Heaney's work here shows how conscious he is of this pivotal (and many-layered) fact of 'responsibility', how he is aware of the *second* part of Auden's by now over-used phrase, 'Poetry makes nothing happen.' For what Auden goes on to say of poetry is that 'it survives; a way of happening, a mouth.' It is poetry as *a way of happening* (and, I'd add, 'for good'), poetry as survivor, that the essays and lectures in this carefully culled selection reveal and celebrate. Between them they show what is most significant about the image of that child in his green nest, weeping at the sound of his own name being called: for the most important fact is that he answered, that he has gone on answering, being answerable.

***

'Objective, informed and lively poetry criticism is a good deal more scarce than it ought to be', says Dennis O'Driscoll in one of the pieces included in *Troubled Thoughts, Majestic Dreams*, his *Selected Prose Writings*. Happily for us, he is himself a marvellous exception to this rule. If one were to compose a portrait of the ideal poetry reviewer, it would contain, I believe (aside from the invaluable, editor-pleasing ability to get the job done on time and within the allotted space), many of the following qualities: the reviewer would be articulate, intelligent, well informed; fluent, smart, witty; enthusiastic for the word, for poems, for poetry; candid, honest, independent, unafraid of the cliques, whatever they might be; always a genuinely curious *student* of literature; always open to what's being done in the middle or at the cutting edge, and always ready to respond in a positive but undeceived way to it. As this generous selection of his work as a reviewer over the past 25 years shows, O'Driscoll possesses all of these qualities to a remarkable degree. Since he began writing for *Hibernia* in 1977, he has produced a regular and regularly impressive list of reviews, along with a few larger review-essays, for the most prominent literary periodicals in Ireland (*Poetry Ireland Review, Irish University Review, Krino, Graph, Tracks*), in England (*London Review of Books, TLS, Poetry Review, Agenda, PN Review, Thumbscrew, London Magazine*), in Europe (*Metre*), and in America (*Poetry, Harvard Review, Southern Review*). It's an impressive list, and the reviews themselves deserve the new permanence that this substantial Gallery collection grants them.

O'Driscoll is an omnivorous reader, a fluent enthusiast, a rare mix of innocence (by which I mean the capacity for curiosity and wonder) and experienced good sense in his approach to poems. Among some other indispensable reviewer's gifts he can claim are the ability to make clean, unadorned, unevasive summaries of a poet's virtues and vices, and the ability to distil the substantive and formal matter of a text into brief, manageable formulations. By striking intuitively and quickly to the heart of any text, and by locating with psychological acuity the main motivations of a writer, O'Driscoll is able to communicate and judge what a writer is trying to do, what he or she is at, how successful the particular achievement, and how worthwhile these aims, ambitions and achievements are. He will remind us, for example, that Kinsella 'is a low-key but very touching chronicler of domestic life and love', while also acknowledging 'the disenchanted severity of his vision.' He can, in a thoroughly researched longer piece on Berryman in Ireland, draw our attention to the American's 'sinewy syntax-driven style' as well as the 'gain in clarity and [a] loss of density in the later "Dream Songs." ' In a richly revealing essay on the work of R.S. Thomas, he observes that 'Thomas's painting poems are at their best as voice-afters rather than voice-overs, when written not in the heat of observation but in the reflective afterglow.' What I also like about O'Driscoll's work is the way, even at its most serious, it can tinge a deep observation with an ironic aside. So Thomas's 'love of the Impressionists surely owes something to the contrast between their dazzling outpourings of light and his own more mildewed climate.' Whether he is discussing the American Robert Hass, the Irish Valentine Iremonger, the Polish Wislawa Szymborska, or the English Philip Larkin, O'Driscoll has invariably some revealing, specific point to make, a point couched in the idioms of description as well as evaluation, a point that is likely to arouse in any half-awake reader a curiosity about the subject, an appetite to go (in a more informed state of mind) to the source. His is a distinctly civilized voice, dealing in distinctly unmystifying ways with the often (as it is commonly perceived) 'difficult' subject of poetry. In his strongly pragmatic commonsense mode, he good-humouredly resists mystification, and enthusiastically makes the matter and the manners of poetry a fact of ordinary life. In his enthusiasms and his candour he is a fine teacher – coaxing readers to become both judicious and experimental, encouraging us to engage more deeply at the level of the individual poem, and to broaden in general our poetry perspectives and horizons. He is not bound to any single point of view, not affiliated with any school of theory or practise. He is faithfully his own man when he says that 'the critic no less than the poet must be a chameleon. Fixed positions are fatal to both .'

An additional reason to value *Troubled Thoughts, Majestic Dreams* is for its inclusion of a number of autobiographically tilted pieces, among them an informative interview (offering a ground of principles and beliefs on which the reviews come to stand: 'poetry, for me, is a private and spontaneous pursuit, not one which is communal or induced', for example, or 'to inscribe in language some hitherto unexpressed area of experience…is worthwhile'), and an instructive collection of *Obiter Poetica*, ('Poetry: the ephemeral in pursuit of the eternal'). There is also a fine synoptic essay – 'A Map of Contemporary Irish Poetry' – in which he manages to touch, if briefly, most of the sites of importance, make quick and incisive pen-sketches of many poets, and note some of the larger landscape features (such as North-South relations).

Fascinated by what he calls poetry politics ('po-biz' its commonly dismissive name), O'Driscoll offers – in 'Troubled Thoughts: *Poetry Politics in Contemporary Ireland*' – a few salutary slaps at 'the stifling bell-jar of Irish literary life' (small pie, to change the metaphor, lots of hungry mouths). He also delivers himself of a thought or three on the 'workshop' phenomenon, and on the issue of poets who earn their living by teaching. In his account of this, as it occurs in Ireland and (mostly) in America, he is mostly caustic and for the most part (like Dana Gioia in America) rather reductive, caricaturing it rather than – as in the case of his response to poetry itself – working deeply inside what he, at firsthand, deeply knows. While his observations on the 'profession' of poetry and its connection with teaching are always sharp and entertaining ('Poetry is an increasingly parthenogenetic art in which poets earn their living by producing new poets'), they often stem from a partial knowledge of the field. His accounts of and reactions to the boom in poets-as-teachers (not only in America) often lack the kind of genial talent for discrimination unfailingly on display in the reviews themselves. A civil servant himself, the difficulty of trying to maintain a (mostly unpaid) career as a poet and writer while holding a 'day job' is very present to him. But in his eagerness to make distinctions between such a job and the work done by teachers, he makes the common enough mistake of assuming the world of the 'school' – whatever school it might be—is somehow not the 'real' world in the way the world of the 'office' is. But, speaking as a teacher, I'd naturally have to say that the work of teachers – even the narrower category of 'writer-teachers' or 'poet-teachers' – takes place in as real a world of human action as any other. Leaving aside the difference in 'holiday' time – mostly used by the teachers I've known to do what's needed to ensure they keep their job – almost anyone writing poems has to make (with the same kind of effort people in most other jobs have to apply to it) the time to do so. But comparisons, as the man said, are odious. And unnecessary. The point is the value of what happens in a piece of writing, not, in the end, the conditions under which it's written. Most teacher poets, in America at least, spend most of their time teaching introductory literature courses to first- or second-year students. To be drowned under a flood of office memoranda is no more worthy or tragic a drowning than to be lost under a deluge of freshman papers on the animal imagery in a love poem by Wyatt. What's important is the quality of response to the choices we, as poets who – like everyone else – have to earn a living, have made. And that response is as various as the individuals making it.

This disagreement aside (and the way O'Driscoll advances his side of the debate is more entertaining than my response to it), and except for the occasional bit of over-praising (Simon Armitage's 'prodigious talents'?, W.S. Graham as 'the supreme comic poet of our time'?) I go back to *Troubled Thoughts, Majestic Dreams* with the pleasure any reader would feel in the vicinity of this serious, congenially expert guide and judge. For what O'Driscoll has gathered here is as rich a compendium of literary judgements, extending over an impressively broad area of poetic experience, both particular and general, as we're likely to encounter. And this collection of mainly critical prose is beautifully book-ended by an affectionate, humorous, minutely detailed memoir evoking the town of Thurles and his own growing up in it, and by a brilliantly constructed personal collage on the photowork of Christian Boltanski. In the memoir, O'Driscoll shows the genesis not only of that engaged yet slightly askance perspective and point of view which serves him so well as a critic, but also demonstrates that love of particulars, their practical vivacity, which informs his reviews and makes them such useful and satisfying points of entry into poems and poets. In the concluding Boltanski piece, called 'Losers, Weepers', he offers a brisk meditation on death, dying, and what Elizabeth Bishop calls 'the art of losing'. It is an eloquent curtain speech, and in its exactly moving, unsentimental way it serves as a reminder of some unspoken root to O'Driscoll's passion for poetry, his passionate and practical dedication to it as poet and (more to the point here) as reviewer. He writes these 'reviews that stay news' (to twist Pound's definition of poetry a bit) in order that their subjects will not be lost. He gives them his generous attention so it will be a question not of 'Losers , Weepers' but (to borrow the title from Seamus Heaney's collection of prose – dedicated to Dennis O'Driscoll and Julie O'Callaghan) of 'Finders, Keepers'. In their judicious enthusiasm, their telling engagement with whatever takes his fancy, O'Driscoll's 'objective, informed and lively' reviews make him an exemplary citizen in the republic of letters, a true, shrewd-tongued but never uncivil, servant of the Muse.

Peter Sirr

Ways of Making

Pearse Hutchinson, *Collected Poems*, Gallery Books, pb., €17.50
Trevor Joyce, *with the first dream of fire they hunt the cold*, New
Writers' Press/Shearsman Books, pb., €16.45

These two books collect substantial bodies of works by two poets
who share a country and a language, but whose ways of making
poems or of coming to poetry have little in common: a fact which in
itself, in a properly diverse poetry culture, should be welcomed. As it
is – and this is one of the dullnesses of division – readers of Joyce are
probably not often readers of Hutchinson, and vice versa.

Pearse Hutchinson comes out of a Fifties-Dublin poetry culture
which is adventurous, loose-limbed, interested in social, political and
sensual alternatives to Ireland. He belongs to the same generation as John
Montague, Thomas Kinsella, Richard Murphy and Anthony Cronin.
There's an elective affinity between his work and that of his co-editors at
Cyphers, Macdara Woods, Eiléan Ní Chuilleanáin and Leland Bardwell.
Michael Hartnett and Paul Durcan would figure in the same company, as
would John Jordan. The context, therefore, is of a rich poetry culture with
a strong modernist / experimental streak, though one which is also allied
to the notion of poetry as a direct channel of communication.

From the outset Hutchinson's poetry was one of strong lines and
definite gestures. The earliest poems here have a clanky rhetoric, with
words and images piled on for effect, the poet choosing to deploy his
full armoury where a single shot might do the job. But he is able to
achieve a real success early on with 'The Nuns at the Medical Lecture',
an extraordinarily forceful and convincing poem, all its rhetorical
flourishes closely marshalled and the thing driving on relentlessly,
each line gathering boldness from the success of the previous:

> The nuns at the medical lecture have rose faces
> like babies surprised into wisdom, the clerical students
> passing the pub look slightly scared, but mainly
> serene, the cultured ancient cod in his lamplit room
> lined with the desert fathers and the village idiots
> and the palace pornographs, warms the port in his palm

and remarks that passion rages most after innocence
because it is innocent, and rages to corrupt. . .

The poems have a rhetorical harshness relieved by the encounter
with the foreign, specifically Spain; the poems attempt to contain the
emotional and sensual otherness unavailable in Ireland, 'The scent of
unseen jasmine on the warm night beach' ('Malaga'). This Spain of the
mind is 'A liberation from green fields':

> Cicada, chameleon, lagarto:
> exotic names have come to mean
> more than exotic creatures: they mean Spain:
> a youthful healing of some northern shame...
> > – 'This Country'

Concern with language is central to the work. At school in the
Forties he studied English, Irish and Latin, and this triple encounter
shaped his sensibility profoundly, although he had first to escape
Ireland and discover Europe before re-discovering Irish in Kevin Street
Public Library. He has written in Irish (these poems and his own
translations of them are published in *The Soul that Kissed the Body*), and
his work in English is informed by Irish as it is by other languages:
words from other languages pepper the poetry, slipped in not as exotic
intruders but as an intrinsic part of the Hutchinson linguistic contin-
uum, its doors open to English, Irish, Spanish, Catalan and Galicio-
Portuguese. That cultural openness and hospitality is one of the most
attractive qualities of the work. It's also, of course, a political gesture;
again and again the poems articulate anger at the threat to languages
and minority cultures:

> And will the black sticks of the devil, Eoghan,
> ever pipe us into heaven at last –
> as one night down the torchlit street of Áth Dara –
> into a heaven of freedom to give
> things back
> > their true names?

> Like streets in Barcelona,
> like Achnasheen,
> Belfast
> > > – 'Achnasheen'

or 'To kill a language is to kill a people', as 'The Frost is All Over' has it.

In Ireland, Hutchinson looks to Irish and traditional music as part of his search for an authentic, non-puritan homeland, a country of poetry and the imagination. 'Fleadh Cheoil' is typical of Hutchinson's approach: part journalistic description, part acute social analysis and part celebration of forces which somehow defy their surroundings. The music soars over the mean streets 'for once taking all harm out – / from even the bunting's pathetic blunderings, / and the many mean publicans making money fast, / hand over fat fist...' In poems like this and 'Gaeltacht', he looks closely and with evident sympathy both at the expressions of culture he's at home with: music, the Irish language and at the social or political circumstances that threaten them. In the case of 'Fleadh Cheoil', the music and the passion that underlies its playing emerge in seeming defiance of the surrounding drabness; in 'Gaeltacht' the speakers of the language are isolated by their poverty, looked down on by the petty bourgeois 'because they / speak in Irish, eat periwinkles, keep / small black porry cattle...' Emigration casts its shadow over both: the fate of many is still 'over there'.

The success of the poems is their reliance on the real and their hard-edged tone. In general, Hutchinson's strengths are more evident when he's focused on an external situation, where his descriptive, observational skills carry the force of the feeling. Some of the poems can be hit and miss; they're often written with real feeling but they are too baldly told, too close to the personal circumstances out of which they're written. But again and again he hits on a distinctive music in poems like 'Boxing the Fox', 'Into their true gentleness', 'Homage to José Martí' or 'Like Trees, like Islands':

> I kneel to fasten your shoes.
> I kneel, creaking, clicking.
> We seem near.
> Blade, thong, buckle.
> I know by which notch
> takes easy entry
> how swollen, how tired, how rested.
> How near we seem — like trees, like islands.
> Like trees on their neighbouring islands
> that cannot uproot themselves and walk —
> no kneeling fingers —
> on water to meet. . .
>
> – 'Like trees, like islands'

At almost three hundred pages this book collects an impressively varied body of work, with the poet's collected translations, mainly from Catalan and Galicio-Portuguese still to come.

***

In his recent book on Irish poetry (*Irish Poetry Since 1950: From Stillness into History*), John Goodby has written of the separation between Irish neo-modernist and mainstream poetries which he finds 'greater, at an insititutional level, in Ireland than in either Britain or the USA, with their relationship characterized not so much by polemic as by ignorance and outright dismissal.' I'm not sure what's meant by 'insititutional level'; it seems to me that the ignorance and dismissal comes from poets and critics on both sides of an artificial though apparently compelling divide. Yet the more interesting point Goodby makes is that 'at the same time, arguably, the gap between the practices of some "mainstream" poets and certain neo-modernists is narrower than elsewhere.' Kinsella, Carson, McGuckian, Muldoon, Ní Chuilleanáin may well inhabit different regions of the contemporary map, but they share a willingness to disrupt, reinvent and shape their worlds according to their own radical poetics. This book, which collects Trevor Joyce's work from 1966 to 2000, should provide an impetus to a further redrawing of that map and a blurring of divisions which serve little purpose other than encourage a culture of coteries.

The first thing that strikes about this work is its range, in terms of subject and formal approach. There are tightly constructed short poems, complex sequences, prose poems, poems which present and add to poems by other poets. The first thing presented is his fascinating working of Buile Shuibhne, a spare, anguished version of the medieval Irish source material from O'Keefe's Irish Text Society version, done many years before Heaney's better known but in no way superior 'Sweeney Astray':

> God has given me life;
>
> without music, without rest,
> without woman's company,
> loveless
> he gave me life,

and so you find me here
living disgraced in Ros Bearaigh;
the life God gave
seems somehow dislocated.

You do not wish to know me.
                    – *The Poems of Sweeny, Peregrine* (I)

Joyce's versions combine the fragmentary and the definite: a language that's gritty, unpredictable, from a perspective that's scattered, demented yet in its way fully in control of its own environment; Sweeney is the *gealt* in flight from the world who sees and experiences with fierce exactness:

In summertime the blue-grey herons stand
rigid above sharp waters.
                    – *The Poems of Sweeny, Peregrine* (IX)

Water; light through green glass,
wind bright as glancing steel,
the ouzel sips the vivid spring,
cress green as the ocean's ice.
                    – *The Poems of Sweeny, Peregrine* (XIII)

The early poems from *Pentahedron* have a steely dispassionate surface, subjecting the visible particulars to close examination. They combine a detachment of tone with a relish for the music of the factual:

Eggshells of white hoar cracked underfoot.
                    – 'River Tolka and Botanical Gardens'

The river, between bridges, lies rectangular,
A sheet of filthy linen, green on grey cement.
                    – 'Gulls on the River Liffey'

These poems are a series of densely textured mini-chronicles, songs that 'some of us made.../about the journey in our minds', and at the same time a poetry of scientific apprehension, as in a poem like 'Construction', which moves from a view of a street to a study of a single cobble. It's an urban poetry that almost seems to write itself from inside the city's stones. It sees the city with extraordinary clarity and condenses it into its essential components so that it doesn't seem to belong to any particular time:

> I know these streets,
> as crammed with dream as a clock with time;
> yellow groundsel through the broken flags
> grows into the mouths of children:
> even the stone ages.
>
> — 'Pentahedron', V

In 'The Turlough', from the later sequence *stone floods*, the poet is geologist and physicist, looking at the occurrence of winter lakes as well as contemplating the expanding universe. What's interesting about a poem like this is how it combines modes of language to produce a kind of forensic lyricism. Joyce always keeps to the fore the pleasure of the line, and the book is full of lines which announce themselves with a sonic flourish and a nod to a lyric tradition remote from this work's intentions but running like a buried current beneath it: 'The jaded sun lies low in his halt galaxy', 'Hammers of ice strike through the chiming earth', 'Above the fog a gibbous moon is growing'.

As the work develops, there's an increasing interest in and reliance on systems, schemes, games where a determining formal element is the play between randomness and order. Joyce likes to take material from arcane sources, scholarly texts, snatches of poetry, proverbs, phrases found in newspapers or overheard, and then to arrange them in seemingly random patterns, in sequences partially explicated via elaborate notes which are themselves elements of the strategy. To read the notes consecutively is to be offered an encyclopaedist's hoarding of knowledge covering, *inter alia*, geology, astronomy, Chinese history, Tocharian culture, Gnostic arcana, Japanese poetry, software, medieval musical forms, and Hungarian folk-songs.

For all their complexity, his orchestrations stay close to a voiced order: even at their most abstract Joyce's poems retain the texture of a speaking voice. 'Chimaera' presents 'a composite, for three voices, plaiting the disparate ghosts of Richard Lovelace, Aloysius Bertrand

and the original authors and later interpolators of the Lie-zi.' The note that explains this also reminds us that 'there is interference on all channels.' Plaiting disparate voices is what many of the poems do, playing off one against another or reacting to the work of other poets. In 'Joinery' a poem by Michael Smith forms part of the fabric; other poems deploy poems by Randolph Healy or Tom Raworth, and are conceived 'with and for' these poets. 'Dark Senses Parallel Street' presents Tom Raworth's poem 'Dark Senses' on the left, and a parallel poem by Joyce on the right which can be read separately or in conjunction with the Raworth poem, continuing across from each Raworth line and forming a whole line of exactly eight words. The sequence 'Trem Neul' is a sustained echoing of and response to many voices. Its epigraph from Yeats – 'All that is personal soon rots; it must be packed in ice or salt' – could serve as manifesto for the whole book. The constant interweaving of voices, their diversity and fragmentariness, the conjunction of randomness and order, are part of an aesthetic which refuses the comforts of the single perspective and the biographical imperatives which drive so much poetry.

This book collects work since 1966, but about three-quarters of it consists of poems written in the last seven or so years, witness to a quite remarkable flowering of Joyce's talent. The work is consistently interesting, formally engaging, wide ranging and risky: altogether an unmissable collection.

Notes on Contributors

Michael S. Begnal lives in Galway. A poet, he is also editor of the literary magazine *The Burning Bush*.

Denise Blake has been published in *The SHOp*, *Stinging Fly* and *Poetry Ireland Review*. She has an M.A. from Lancaster University/ Poet's House; is a member of Errigal Writers; and translates the poetry of Cathal Ó Searcaigh.

Anthony Cronin's first collection of poems appeared in London in 1958; numerous other volumes have followed. As well as being a poet, he is a comic novelist, literary critic, social commentator, broadcaster, and biographer (of Flann O'Brien and Samuel Beckett). He has been editor of a number of literary magazines and received many awards. He was responsible for establishing Aosdána, the Irish state body which funds writers, artists and musicians.

Franz Fassbind, a German-speaking Swiss, was born in 1919. He studied music and became an accomplished composer. It was literature, however, to which he finally devoted himself and in which he has won recognition. He was accorded successive literary awards: in 1943 the Prize of Radio Zurich; in 1955 the F. Meyer Prize; and in 1981 the Inner Schweiz Prize. The imprint Olten & Freiburg im Breisgau: Walter Verlag, has brought out twelve volumes of Fassbind's *Collected Works*, including novels, short stories, stage and radio plays, journalism, and poetry, both epic and lyric.

Tony Frazer is the editor of Shearsman Books.

Eamon Grennan teaches at Vassar College, and was the 2002 Heimbold Professor of Irish Studies at Villanova University. His most recent books are *Still Life with Waterfall*, and *Facing the Music: Irish Poetry in the 20th Century*.

Randolph Healy was born in Scotland in 1956, his family moving to Dublin eighteen months later. He has published *25 Poems* (1983); a pamphlet, *Envelopes* (1966); and most recently a series of chapbooks, *Rana Rana!*, *Arbor Vitae*, *Flame*, *Scales*, and *Daylight Saving Sex*. Also a mathematician, he lives in Wicklow from where he runs Wild Honey Press. A *Selected Poems* is forthcoming from Salt.

Seamus Heaney was born in 1939 in County Derry. He was awarded the Nobel Prize in Literature in 1995.

Fanny Howe was born in Buffalo, New York, in 1940, daughter of the Irish writer, Mary Manning. Her recent collections of poetry include *Selected Poems* (2000), *Forged* (1999), and *Q* (1998). She is also author of several novels, including *Nod* (1998), several short story collections, and books for young adults. She was recipient of the 2001 Lenore Marshall Poetry Prize for her *Selected Poems*, and has won awards from the National Endowment for the Arts, The National Poetry Foundation, the California Council for the Arts, and the *Village Voice*, among others. She currently lives in Massachusetts.

David Lloyd was born in Dublin. He has published a number of volumes of poetry and literary criticism, the latest of which is *Anomalous States*.

Lorna Reynolds is retired Professor of English Literature in University College, Galway. Previously she taught for many years in the Department of English in University College, Dublin. She edited the *University Review*, which under her editorship offered an important outlet for many poets.

Maurice Scully was born in Dublin in 1952. Editor of *The Beau*, Beau Press and Coelacanth Press, his recent books include *Steps* and *5 Freedoms of Movement*. He issued a recent CD entitled *Mouthpuller*. *Livelihood*, a long work in five books composed between 1986 and 1998, is due as a single volume later this year from Wild Honey Press.

Peter Sirr is the Director of the Irish Writers' Centre. His latest collection, *Bring Everything*, was published by Gallery in 2000.

Michael Smith, co-founder of the New Writers' Press, is the current editor of *Poetry Ireland Review*.

Books Received

Mention here does not preclude a review in a future issue.

Pearse Hutchinson, *Collected Poems*, Gallery Books.
John O'Rourke, *Glimpses – As seen Through a Veil: Poems 1986-2001*.
Selected by Michael Longley, *20th-Century Irish Poems*, Faber & Faber.
Ed. by David Pike, *Pulsar: Poems from Ligden Poetry Society*, March 2002, Edition 1/02 (29).
Ed. by Paul D. Reich, *Sycamore Review*, Volume 14, Number 1, Winter/Spring 2002.
Ian Hamilton, *Against Oblivion: Some lives of the Twentieth Century Poets*, Viking.
Ed. by Kevin Bailey, *The Haiku Quarterly*, Numbers 23 & 24.
Matthew James Ould, *Searching For The Light*, Paper Doll.
David Harsent, *Marriage*, Faber & Faber.
Ed. by Christopher Howell, *Willow Springs*, Number 49, January 2002.
Peter Robinson, *The Great Friend*, Worple Press.
John Jones, *Carreg Las & Other Work*, The Collective Press.
Federico García Lorca, translated by Michael Smith, *The Tamarit Poems*, Dedalus.
Paddy Bushe, *In Ainneoin na gCloch*, Coiscéim.
Cliodna Cussen, *Sifíní*, Coiscéim.
Dolores Stewart, *'Sé Sin le Rá*, Coiscéim.
Ed. by Merryn Williams, *In the Spirit of Wilfred Owen: A New Anthology of Poems*, The Wilfred Owen Association.
Ed. by Jonathan and Jessica Wordsworth, *The New Penguin Book of Romantic Poetry*, Penguin Books.
Brendan Kennelly, *The Little Book of Judas*, Bloodaxe Books.
Tim Cunningham, *Don Marcelino's Daughter*, Peterloo Poets.
Ed. by Herbert Leibowitz, *Parnassus*, Vol. 26, No. 1.
Ed. by Pierre Dubrunquez, *poésie*, no. 91/février 2002.
Edward MacKinnon, *Wising Up, Dressing Down*, Shoestring Press.
Hubert Moore, *Touching Down In Utopia*, Shoestring Press.
Graham Holderness, *Craeft*, Shoestring Press.
Fred Johnston, *Being Anywhere: New & Selected Poems*, Lagan Press.
Fred Bazler, *I Once Saw My Heart*, Minerva Press.
John Brown, *In the Chair: Interviews with Poets from the North of Ireland*, Salmon Publishing.
Ed. by Thomas McCarthy, *The Turning Tide: New Writing from County Waterford*.
Seamus Heaney, *Finders Keepers: Selected Prose 1971-2001*, Faber & Faber.
Brian Waltham, *The Soldier On The Pier*, Peterloo Poets.
Ed. by Leo Regan, *Flaming Arrows*, Issue 7, 2002.
Orlando Ricardo Menes, *Rumba atop the Stones*, Peepal Tree Press.

Peter Carpenter, *The Black-Out Book*, Arc Publications.
Ed. by James S. Donnelly Jr. & Vera Kreilkamp, *Éire-Ireland*, Fall/Winter 2001.
Gerard Smyth, *Daytime Sleeper*, Dedalus.
Nicholas Cummins, *The Bell Sound: Castleknock Poems*, Castleknock College Press.
Ed. by Deborah Tall, *Seneca Review*, Vol XXXII, No. 1, Spring 2002.
Ed. by Robert Minhinnick, *Poetry Wales*, Volume 37, Number 3, 2002. [Incorrectly listed in *PIR 72* as the Winter 2002 issue].
Ed. by Robert Minhinnick, *Poetry Wales*, Volume 37, Number 4, Spring 2002.
Vernon Scannell, *Of Love & War: New and Selected Poems*, Robson Books.
Gearóid MacLochlainn, *Stream Of Tongues / Sruth Teangacha*, Cló Iar-Chonnachta.
Ed. by Michael Begnal, *The Burning Bush*, Number Seven, Spring 2002.
Vona Groarke, *Flight*, Gallery Books.
Ed. by David Hamilton, *The Iowa Review*, Volume Thirty-Two, Number One, Spring 2002.
Madison Morrison, *Magic*, The Working Week Press.
Ron Phelps, *The Sentence of Madison Morrison*, Sentence of the Gods Press.
Ed. by Daniel Veach, *Atlanta Review*, Volume VIII, Issue Number 2.
Ed. by Peter Forbes, *Poetry Review*, Volume 92, No. 1, Spring 2002.
E.A. Markham, *A Rough Climate*, Anvil Press.
Ed. by Patricia Oxley, *acumen Literary Journal*, No. 43, May 2002.
Bert Hornback, *Talking About Poetry*, Bellarmine University Press.
Patrick Cotter, *The True Story of Aoife and Lir's Children & Other Poems*, Three Spires Press.
Ed. by Pierre Dubrunquez, *poésie*, no. 92 / avril 2002.
Ed. by Brenda Miller, *Bellingham Review*, Volume XXV, No. 1, issue #50.
John Brannigan, *Brendan Behan: Cultural Nationalism and the Revisionist Writer*, Four Courts Press.
Ed. by Mary O'Donnell, *Away From The Tribe: Selected Poems of the Bealtaine Writers' Group*.
Bernie Kenny, *Poulnabrone*.
Somhairle MacGill-Eain/Sorley MacLean), *Dáin do Eimhir/Poems To Eimhir* (ed. by Christopher Whyte), The Association for Scottish Literary Studies.
Ed. by Anthony W. Butler, *Garm Lu – A Canadian Arts Journal*, Éarrach 2002.
Gerard Hanberry, *Rough Night*, Stonebridge.
ROPES (Review of Postgraduate Studies), Issue Ten, Spring 2002, NUI, Galway.
John O'Donnell, *Some Other Country*, Bradshaw Books.
Ed. by Daphne Dwyer, *Mindful Men*, Bradshaw Books.
Fred Marchant, *House on Water, House in Air*, Dedalus.
Ed. by Declan Barron, *eurochild 2002: Poetry & Artwork by Young People*, Eurochild International Project.

Ed. by Sebastian Barker, *The London Magazine*, April/May 2002.

Ed. by Chris Agee & Cathal O'Searcaigh, *Irish Pages – A Journal of Contemporary Writing*.

Sheenagh Pugh, *The Beautiful Lie*, seren.

Sarah Corbett, *the witch bag*, seren.

Ed. by Rob Schouten & Robert Minhinnick, *In a Different Light: Fourteen contemporary Dutch-language poets*, seren.

Paul Groves, *wowsers*, seren.

Vuyelwa Carlin, *Marble Sky*, seren.

Ed. by Les Merton, *Poetry Cornwall*, Volume 1, Number 2, 2002.

John McGuckian, *Talking with My Brother*, Summer Palace Press.

Gráinne Tobin, *Banjaxed*, Summer Palace Press.

Pamela Greene, *Tattoo Me*, Summer Palace Press.

Ed. by Adrian Rice & Angela Reid, *A Conversation Piece: Poetry and Art*, The National Museums and Galleries of Northern Ireland in association with Abbey Press.

Ed. by Pierre Dubrunquez, *poésie*, No. 93/juin 2002.

Moyra Donaldson, *Beneath The Ice*, Lagan Press.

Alice Oswald, *Dart*, Faber & Faber.

Katie O'Loughlin, *I Can't Pull it Together Enough to Look Like my Poster*, Guest House Press 2002.

Ed. by Ingrid de Kok, *Carapace 37*, June 2002.

Karen Press, *The Coffee Shop Poems*, SnailPress.

Patrick Cullinan, *Transformations*, Carapace Poets.

Tatamkhulu Afrika, *Mad Old Man Under The Morning Star: (the poet at eighty)*, SnailPress.

Ed. by Christopher Cahill, *The Recorder*, Volume 15, No.1, Spring 2002.

Ed. by Henri Deluy, *Action Poétique*, 167/168. Sommaire 2002.

Simon Armitage, *The Universal Home Doctor*, Faber & Faber.

Simon Armitage, *Travelling Songs*, Faber & Faber.

David Hart, *Crag Inspector*, Five Seasons Press.

Ed. by Robert Minhinnick, *Poetry Wales*, Volume 38, Number 1, Summer 2002.

Ann Davidson, *Songs for the Brave*, scw books.

Daniel Thomas Moran, *From HiLo to Willow Pond: New & Selected Poems*, Street Press.

Ed. by Asher Weill, *Ariel: The Israeli Review of Arts and Letters*, May 2002.

Ed. by Stephanie McKenzie & Marc Thackray, *Humber Mouths: Young Voices from the west coast of Newfoundland & Labrador*, Scop Productions Inc.

Previous Editors of *Poetry Ireland Review*